i

ii

Dream Gardener

Bertrand H. Farr

FARR'S MATCHLESS PEONIES

CAMERON

BERTRAND H. FARR
WYOMISSING, PENNA.

Back cover of 1909 catalog

FARR'S HARDY PLANTS

JUNIATA

GLORY OF READING

WYOMISSING

BERTRAND H FARR

MONTEZUMA

WYOMISSING
PENNSYLVANIA

Inset: Front cover of 1909 catalog. Farr's iris fields from a glass slide. View looking east toward City of Reading and Mount Penn

2

A CORNER OF ONE OF FARR'S PEONY FIELDS WYOMISSING, JUNE 10, 1909.

Page from Farr's 1909 catalog

Dream Gardener

Pioneer Nurseryman
Bertrand H. Farr

George H. Edmonds

Dream Gardener:

Pioneer Nurseryman Bertrand H. Farr

George H. Edmonds

© 2008
GHE BOOKS

Manufactured in the United States of America

ISBN: 978-0-615-23865-4

Designed by Ellen Hardy
Printed by Flagship Press, Inc.

*To the gardeners,
who beautify the world*

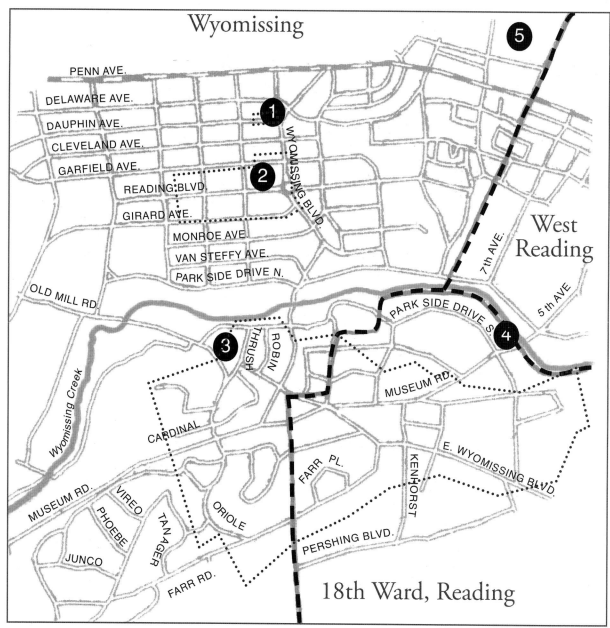

Dotted areas designate the approximate lands Bertrand Farr used, leased and/or owned for his nursery at one time or another from 1897 to 1924.

CURRENT MAP OF PARTS OF
WYOMISSING, WEST READING
AND THE 18th WARD, READING

KEY:
1. Farr residence, 118 Wyomissing Boulevard
2. Farr Nursery office and greenhouse, 1250 Garfield Avenue
3. Farr's "Dream Garden" area
4. Reading Public Museum
5. Wyomissing Industries (Textile Machine Works, Berkshire Knitting Mills, and Narrow Fabric Co.)

TABLE OF CONTENTS

INTRODUCTION

One hundred years ago in 1908, Bertrand H. Farr issued his first nursery catalog for the American public. He was not yet ready to call himself a nurseryman despite the large number of plants he was offering in this catalog. Nevertheless, this catalog was the major step to Farr's becoming famous as a pioneer nurseryman. He would be called "the real pioneer of the American Iris." He would be recognized as the man who introduced the bearded iris into the United States. The man who also hybridized and introduced over 50 new irises and who helped to popularize the iris and many other hardy plants like peonies, daylilies, phloxes and delphiniums.

Although "Better Plants By Farr" did not become Farr's business slogan for his catalog titles until his last years, these words could have served from the beginning to define both his self-confidence and his high standards. His earlier catalogs had the more modest titles "Farr's Hardy Plants" and, later, "Farr's Hardy Plant Specialties." With "Better Plants By Farr," Farr intended to point to an ideal, to a constant striving for improvement. He and his nursery associates would strive, as he wrote, "for better cultivation, better packing and shipping, better and more prompt service in the office, and most important, to select for the inexperienced gardener, out of the hundreds of varieties in the trade, those which will give the most satisfactory results and the ones really worth while."

In his time, Bertrand Farr won many medals for his plant collections, some of which were the largest in the nation. He was an active member of the American Peony Society, American Iris Society, American Rose Society, Pennsylvania Nurserymen's Association and Eastern Nurserymen's Association. He became internationally famous as a nurseryman. However, in modern times knowledge of him and his contributions to American horticulture have faded, even in his home areas of Iowa and Pennsylvania.

Born in 1931, just seven years after Farr's death, I grew up in the Pennsylvania town of Wyomissing, a suburb of Reading, where Farr spent the last half of his life and had his nursery. Through the years, from Massachusetts, I have stayed in touch with Wyomissing and recently published a book about its unusual suburban development and industrial history, but gave only slight attention to Farr and his achievements.

In this book I want to make up for that neglect and tell his story for the many who know virtually nothing about him as well as for those who know only his life's outlines. (There are some horticulturists today who are familiar with Farr and who keep records of some of his plants and even still grow them.) In my research I have found important and interesting materials never published before and much material not easily accessible.

In this latter category are the remarkable catalogs Farr published between 1908 and 1924. From these catalogs, the reader will soon discover, I have frequently quoted passages to enable Farr to speak in his own words. These passages, from personal essays and even poems about his life and his beloved plants, I found to be the sources most revealing about him as a human being. Since his catalogs also provide evidence of what was known to be Farr's obsessive desire to have really large (if not the largest) collections of plants, I have counted the numbers of some plants and provided the results. Also, I have included many photos as well as some decorative plant symbols from Farr's catalogs.

At the time of Farr's death, he was in the process of moving his nursery 12 miles away to another town. Then the business was sold and resold at least two more times over the years so that the remaining records were limited except for the complete catalog collection. Other materials about him that were collected shortly after his death by the American Iris and the American Peony Societies and now reside in their archives were also helpful for this book. Research in a variety of other places has enabled me to explain Farr's relation to a number of other significant horticultural people, and research for my previous book on Wyomissing has enabled a look at the context of his life there.

I dedicated this book to "The gardeners, who beautify the world" to honor all gardeners, but especially the gardeners who helped me with this horticultural book and the gardeners who have benefited from Bertrand Farr's pioneering work and who have followed in one way or another his enthusiasm for the beautiful in the garden.

—*George H. Edmonds*

Andover, Massachusetts
May 2008

Late 1890's view of the conjunction of Wyomissing and Reading Boulevards as they form "The Circle" with the Farr residence (middle, white house) and vacant areas to the left, where Farr grew peonies

Chapter 1

Transformation

It seems like yesterday, though many years have slipped away, since there was a boy's garden out on the western prairie; then the city where there was no garden – only a memory of a garden that was, or a dream of a garden to be. Then came Wyomissing, and a man's garden which was an unrestrained passion for growing things soon filled until it overflowed out into the open fields, a riot of glorious color, an intoxication of delight, like the promise of the rainbow fulfilled.

—Bertrand H. Farr
Catalog, Fifth Edition, 1915

Moving to Wyomissing in the last years of the 19th century transformed Bertrand Farr. By the first years of the 20th century, he had become a new man. The move to a new home with garden space unleashed his passions for beautiful flowers and plants and enabled him to emerge as an internationally-famous horticulturist.

In 1891, at the age of 27 and having worked for a few years in Philadelphia, Farr moved 60 miles west to the industrial city of Reading and established a business for himself. In the city's business directory, he is listed as a piano tuner with the address of 438 Penn Street in Reading, also the address of the store of C.W. Edwards selling pianos, organs, music, and musical instruments. Farr had studied piano in his earlier life growing up in Iowa, had attended the New England Conservatory of Music in Boston for two years, and had owned a music business back in Iowa for a short time.

The year 1896 was to mark the turning point in the life of Bertrand Farr, now in his 33rd year. Just a short time earlier, several businessmen in Reading turned themselves into real estate developers by buying up farmland just a mile or two west of the city, formed the Reading Suburban Real Estate Company, and hired an engineer to lay out streets and house lots for what was to become the new suburb of Wyomissing. In quick succession Farr bought three lots on what was becoming Wyomissing Boulevard, one of the two showplace streets in the suburb, and made plans for building one of the first houses in Wyomissing. He also returned to Webster City, Iowa to marry Anna Willis, whom he had met there when he had his music business.

Cover of Farr's first catalog – 1908

Judging by limited factual records, one would not understand that Farr was transforming himself. In the census of 1900, Farr still listed himself as a piano tuner. From the Reading business directory for 1904, he had now become part of the Farr & Gerhardt partnership running a store at 809 Penn Street selling pianos, organs, and musical merchandise. Also, according to a biographical account, he had both bought and then sold a music store in nearby Lancaster, Pennsylvania in the early 1900's. In 1905 during the course of a deposition involving the incorporation of Wyomissing, Farr continued to identify himself as being in the piano business.

Now, try to imagine what else Farr had been doing in the 10 or so short years before 1908, when he issued his first catalog of hardy plant specialties, a well-written and designed booklet of 64 pages offering for sale 1,667 different cultivars – yes, 1,667 different hardy plants in sufficient quantity to advertise and sell. First, there were 412 different irises, including Tall Bearded Irises, Dwarf Bearded Irises, Beardless Irises, and Japanese Irises. Included in the major group of Tall Bearded Irises were complete sub-groups that irisarians would relish for their differences in colors, forms, and patterns with intriguing names like Pallida, Variegata, Neglecta, Plicata, and Squalens.

Especially dramatic, however, was Farr's introduction of his own irises, eight new irises that he himself had hybridized and named: **Glory of Reading, Iroquois, Juniata, Leda, Montezuma, Mt. Penn, Windham,** and **Wyomissing.** These Tall Bearded introductions, along with all the other 404 irises he had managed not only to collect from various sources but also to grow in quantity, combined to produce the largest collection of irises in the United States. In his introductory essay to "The Iris" section of this first catalog, Farr writes: "There is a peculiar charm about the Iris that appeals irresistibly to those whose taste for the refined and delicately beautiful leads them to seek a close acquaintance with it." Close acquaintance, indeed!

In his essay introducing the next section of his catalog "The Peony," Farr writes: "The Peony is, above all others, 'the flower for the million and for the millionaire.'" Building on that high-number spirit, his catalog goes on to offer and describe 539 types of peonies. Writing about their historical backgrounds, he mentions their sources from a variety of peony growers

Farr's iris field, photo & caption from Farr's first catalog

TALL BEARDED IRISES — A MASS OF IRIDESCENT COLOR

15

Peony field photos from Farr's first catalog. Photo on right taken from "The Circle" looking north toward Garfield and Cleveland Avenues

in France, especially, and in England, America, and Japan. His catalog offers this abundance of peonies in categories like "New and Rare Peonies from France," "Kelway's New Peonies" [from Langport, England], "Hollis' New Seedling Peonies" [from near Boston, Massachusetts], "Japanese Peonies," and "Tree Peonies."

Farr also states that his peony collection "has been grown and studied for more than eight years before I felt justified in offering it for sale." In his concern for both quality and authenticity, "I was fortunate in discovering, at the outset, the dangers of promiscuous buying, and the greater part of my collection has been imported direct from the establishments of M. Lemoine and M. Dessert, in France, the most famous growers in the world today, and everywhere acknowledged to be the most reliable." Purchases he made in America were "from specialists with whom I am personally acquainted and who I am satisfied have the correct varieties."

Farr was becoming a special expert in peonies through his volunteer work at Cornell University helping to standardize the chaotic condition of peony nomenclature in America. Especially because of multiple names for the same cultivar, it would have been difficult to count the real number of peonies in a nurseryman's collection unless one was as knowledgeable and scrupulous as Farr apparently was. In any case, it is likely that even in his first catalog, Farr also had one of the largest collection of peonies in the country; and, if not the largest then, certainly soon after as his collection continued to grow.

After this initial emphasis in the catalog on Irises and Peonies, a total of 951 cultivars, there are still 28 pages devoted to another 716 cultivars of a large variety of other hardy plants.

The catalog announces "A superb collection embracing the choicest of Lemoine's latest introductions of Phloxes." Delphiniums, "grand and stately" "supply our gardens with a wealth of blue that would be sadly lacking were it not for these magnificent plants." "For dazzling barbaric splendor, the great Oriental poppies are absolutely unrivaled." From Lemoine again, Farr has imported double-flowering lilacs. These lilacs are only the beginning of what later on will become a collection of 150 different lilacs that Farr will donate to the Reading Public Museum and become the basis for a 40-year tradition of "Lilac Sunday" each spring.

Other Farr offerings included Day Lilies, Japanese Anemones, Pyrethrums, Pompom Chrysanthemums, Dahlias (in large numbers), Roses, and "Miscellaneous Shrubs of Special Merit," including Azaleas, Japanese Maples, Rhododendrons, and Mock Oranges.

The accompanying copy of the Index of this first catalog only summarizes the work that Farr accomplished in a very short time, but does give the reader a quick look at the complete list of his plants by major categories.

Photo from Farr's 1920 catalog with the children of Farr's stableman – James Keiser, John Keiser, and Catharine Keiser Reed – with blooms of "Elie Chevalier" peonies

*W*here Farr grew what must have been hundreds of thousands of these plants poses an interesting question not easy to answer because, initially, he did not own much land. This writer, delving into the "magic" of this amazing Farr enterprise, has relied on real estate records, photographs in Farr's catalogs, some guess work, and the memory of one remarkable, elderly woman for answers about Farr's early nursery work. Prior to the time of his first catalog in 1908, the deed records show that Farr had purchased 11 Wyomissing house lots in five transactions from 1896 to 1900. House lots, as created by the Reading Suburban Development Company, were either 25 by 115 feet or 20 by 150 feet, depending on location. Of Farr's 11 lots, more than half were for his home on Wyomissing Boulevard and then later for an office and a long

INDEX

Index from the first catalog

FIELD OF JAPANESE IRIS AT WYOMISSING
As grown in ordinary soil during a dry season without irrigation

Photo &
caption
from the
first catalog

greenhouse on nearby Garfield Avenue. To grow all the plants his catalog offered, Farr must have leased or borrowed nursery space on other house lots and the still-existing open farm land in Wyomissing and abutting townships.

Catharine Keiser Reed, born in 1914, began to live and grow up on a section of Farr's nursery in 1917 when her father, James Keiser, was hired by Farr to take care of his work horses and perform other nursery tasks. As a nonagenarian today, she is active and alert, can recite vigorously from memory poetry she has written, lives in her own home with some help, and only recently in this early 2008 period has given up driving a car. In written letters, several interviews, and a drive around the relevant real estate, she has provided useful clues about the Farr nursery from its days even before she was born.

From all this available evidence, it seems likely that Farr planted near his home on the lots he owned along Garfield Avenue and on leased lots between Garfield and Cleveland Avenues and then along Reading Boulevard (please see map to locate Farr's house on the corner of Wyomissing Boulevard and Dauphin Avenue and neighboring streets just mentioned) and other lots to the south in Wyomissing, and then farther away on much larger pieces of farm land in abutting townships, much of this land later annexed by the Borough of Wyomissing. Farr took advantage of this fertile, former farm land, which, however, was also scattered around in pieces at various distances from each other—some just down the street from Farr's house and others almost two miles away.

Photographs in Farr's first catalog show fairly large fields of his plants, and quoted excerpts from a Reading newspaper report frequent visitors in June 1908: "Wednesday of this week was visitors' day at Mr. Farr's, and hundreds of persons came from near and far to examine the flowers." "The largest collection of peonies, 650 varieties [many more than in the catalog], 100,000 plants, is to be found in the fields of Bertrand Farr, at Wyomissing." "The next feast day after peony time in Bertrand Farr's calendar of beauties has come and reached its height. Mr. Farr's gardens at Wyomissing have been visited by many persons during the past week for a great field of Japanese iris has blossomed magnificently and added its contribution to Mr. Farr's 'feast of weeks,' as we like to call his succession of flowers."

What drove this Mr. Farr, presumably a music man, to create this wonderful horticultural "feast" described in this chapter? Bertrand Farr provides his own answer to this question in the very first paragraph of his first catalog:

> *I take pleasure in presenting herewith the first edition of my catalogue of Hardy Plant Specialties, as it is another step toward the realization of a desire, formed many years ago, to live, and be, among beautiful flowers; to work among them, and be surrounded by them. The call has been instinctive and irresistible, and the complete and final surrender has brought restoration to health and a joy of living that has made it worth while, regardless of any monetary returns.*

Chapter 2

The Early Years

There was a child went forth every day,
And the first object he look'd upon, that object he became,
And that object became part of him for the day or a certain part of the day,
Or for many years or stretching cycles of years.

The early lilacs became part of this child,
And grass and white and red morning-glories, and white and red clover,
and the song of the phoebe-bird....

from *Leaves of Grass*, Walt Whitman

The phrase "regardless of any monetary returns" points to the way Farr's friends would later describe him as a nurseryman "whose love for flowers entirely overshadowed any monetary interest he had in them" and as "first of all a beauty enthusiast and secondarily a business man." For now, this chapter will look in on Farr's early life and some influences on his desire to live and be and work among beautiful flowers.

Although Bertrand H. Farr was born in Windham, Vermont on October 14, 1863, he grew up from the time he was five years old in the Middle West. In Vermont, Farr's father had a mountain-side farm where he raised sheep and produced maple sugar. Farr writes that when he was five years old, his family moved to Wisconsin for about three years, "part of the time at Lake Geneva, and a part in the little seminary town of Rochester near Milwaukee." Here occurred the event that Farr narrates as the seminal moment in his life of loving flowers:

Here I saw my first peony, one of the early flowering, old–fashioned red varieties it was but I thought it mighty fine and was very glad to accept my aunt's proposal to give me one of the blooms if I would go to the pasture and bring the cow home. This led to further negotiations by which I agreed to go after the cow for a week in consideration of her giving me a "piney toe" and so it was I came possessed of my first peony.

Only one peony, but nevertheless the beginning of Farr's later willingness to spend a great deal of money and time for importing, growing and possessing many flowers.

From Wisconsin the family moved again, this time to the middle of Iowa outside of Webster City to an area that later would become Kamrar, where Orlando Farr established a 400-acre cattle farm on the prairie and eight year old Bert began finding the wonders of the prairie land around him. Farr writes that the prairie he knew when a boy was "wild enough but it was beautiful, a literal carpet of the wild flowers." He continues in these moving and revealing paragraphs:

Bertrand Farr, as a young man

Mine is a story of a dream come true; the evolution of a love for the beautiful first awakened in the idyllic days of boyhood when with my Indian pony I used to herd the cattle over the wild prairie, an endless phosphorescent sea of waving green, reflecting the changing colors of myriads of wild flowers, where the dawn came up with the booming thunder of the pheasant and the glad notes of the bobolink came tinkling down out of the noon-day sky.

In the midst of this mysterious nature-land rose a solitary pyramid: itself a mystery, relic, perhaps of a vanished race. Halfway up in the side overlooking a little pond encircled by blue irises, where the red-winged black birds swarmed among the rushes, was an old wolf's den which I enlarged and made mine. Its summit was the center of my universe, where the great plain stretched away until the blue dome of heaven swept down around it and I dreamed of what the future might bring to me beyond this mystic circle.

The cultivated flowers and plants that were to become so important in Farr's future also had a place in his boyhood in Iowa, though evidence is slim. One clue to the Farr family's growing cultivated flowers in Iowa comes from a Webster City newspaper listing Bert's father's

22

having won five prizes at the Hamilton County Agricultural Society Exhibition in 1881 for the best display of dahlias, best 12 blooms, largest verbenas, best flat bouquet, and best round bouquet. Other second-hand evidence comes from a letter written after Farr's death by his sister Nellie (20 years younger than her brother), who wrote that her father had told her "when Bert was a boy at home he always wanted a one fourth of their garden for flowers."

In his later life Bertrand Farr would write several poems and poetic essays, an interest that apparently had an early beginning when Farr, as a teenager, submitted a poem to the Webster City newspaper on the occasion of the death of his baby brother Leslie:

Have You Seen Him?

Lines written on the death of Leslie Farr,
who died August 1st, 1878, aged five months.

Have you seen him? little angel:
   Tell me, oh, ye stars of night.
Have you seen our little "Leslie"
   Flying Heavenward to-night?

Perhaps you chance to meet him,
   Traveling onward in your course,
Going toward the Heavenly city,
   Free from earth and all its cares.

Soon he'll meet the little angels,
   As he gains the silvery shore –
Frank and Flora – still we miss them,
   Darling ones who went before.

Ah! methinks that I see them
   Through faith's vision, clear and bright
As they near the loving Savior
   To receive his crown of light.

See! He smiles upon them sweetly,
   Seated upon His throne on high,
As they timidly draw near him,
   And bids them fear not, "It is I."

If you see him, gentle moonbeams,
   As swiftly on your course you glide,
Tell him we shall miss our "Birdie,"
   'Till we cross the rolling tide.

—BERTRAND FARR

Bert Farr was the second of seven children his parents had, three of whom died quite young. His older brother, Frank, died at age four, and later his sister Florence (Flora in the poem), and then this baby brother, Leslie. Another sister Stella died at age 37 in 1903, and Farr's younger brother Edward died at age 48 in 1922. At Farr's death in 1924, the only surviving sibling of the seven children was Nellie (Mrs. J.O. Crawford, living in Chicago), who died in 1971 at age 87. Although no details have surfaced about Farr's physical condition, after Farr's death two of his friends, using the same words, wrote that Farr was "handicapped by physical infirmity in early life."

Biographical sketches of Farr trace his ancestry five generations back to 1636 when Abraham Farr emigrated from England to Massachusetts. Bert's main line of ancestors remained in New England until his father, Orlando, took the family to the Midwest. Bert's mother, Paulina Holton Farr, was from North Walcott, Vermont.

*W*hen Farr's mother began to notice his artistic sensitivities and talents, she bought a piano and started him on piano lessons. Farr writes, "[In] a very short time I thought I was a musical prodigy and the neighbors all seemed to be of the same opinion." He says that he went to high school in Webster City but also spent a year and a half back in Rochester, Wisconsin "at an invitation of an uncle," attending the local high school called The Rochester Seminary and operated by the Freewill Baptist Church in a converted hotel building. Remarkably, and without any further explanation, he mentions "graduating at the age of seventeen to become an Iowa county school teacher." Then, at age 20, "In the fall of 1883 I went to Boston to study music at the New England Conservatory where I spent two years, just long enough to discover that I was not and never would be a musical prodigy though I studied hard."

The Conservatory archives reveal that Farr attended the school for two years (6 semesters), studying piano with John D. Buckingham and taking four semesters of piano tuning, one of harmony, and one of voice. However, Farr supplemented this formal musical curriculum in Boston with a more significant, though informal, horticultural "curriculum" across the Charles River in Cambridge.

One can imagine what a super-strong magnetic pull lay across the Charles just a two-mile horse-car ride away from downtown Boston – one of the most famous commercial nurseries in 19th century America – and why, as he writes, he "could not resist … the temptation to play hooky and wander over to Cambridge and spend many an afternoon [there]." The Hovey & Co.'s Cambridge Nurseries contained 40 acres and 20 large greenhouses, which, themselves, covered an acre. A variety of sources, especially the Hovey catalogs from Farr's student period in Boston, reveal what Farr could have experienced and learned from: great collections of Camellias and Azaleas "unequaled in this country or Europe"; a collection of Water Lilies that "fills three large aquariums"; over an acre of "hardy Rhododendrons, Azaleas, and Kalmias"; 200 varieties of the "best and newest" Hybrid Perpetual Roses; a collection of 2,000 pear trees containing 300 varieties; and "specimens of Nordmans Spruce, Weeping Beech, Virgilia Lutea, variegated Tulip-Tree, and other rare trees and shrubs." Also, particularly important for Farr's own nursery work in Wyomissing was the Hovey collection of 100 varieties of peony. And these catalog descriptions only begin to suggest the many attractions Hovey & Co. might have had for Farr.

Charles M. Hovey (1810-1887) and his brother Phineas dated the beginning of their formal business from 1834, though Charles began his keen interest in strawberries in 1832 when he started creating and testing many new varieties, as many as 50, one of which he marketed successfully in New England as the "Hovey." At the nursery he expanded his interests and collections to other fruits like grape, plum, apple, and pear. As an author, he became famous for his book *Fruits of America,* issued in two volumes with over 100 colored plates between 1852 and 1856. He "was widely known in the 19th century as one of the country's foremost hybridizers of commercial plants. Among the plants that Hovey successfully hybridized were varieties of arborvitae, strawberries, cherries, pears, camellias, azaleas, lilies, geraniums, and orchid cactus." Charles and his brother also had a business selling a full range of seeds, which they operated from their site in Boston, and annually issued three sets of illustrated catalogs for seeds, bulbs, and greenhouse and bedding plants.

Charles Hovey founded in 1835 *American Gardener's Magazine,* which shortly later became *Magazine of Horticulture,* and was the editor for 34 years of this highly-respected journal covering horticultural information on many subjects like cultivation science, descriptions of new varieties, landscaping ideas, and book reviews. Active in many roles in the Massachusetts Horticultural Society, America's first and most active such society in the 19th century, Hovey served as president in 1863-1866 and was one of many Bostonians aiding the Society's varied horticultural activities. These included frequent public displays of interesting vegetables and flowers in downtown market areas; the New England Flower Show, which had begun in 1828; and the Mount Auburn Cemetery project, a pioneering creation of a combination arboretum and cemetery, which still includes both wild and garden flowers, all on quite hilly terrain.

In Bertrand Farr's brief autobiographical sketch, he writes only that he spent "many an afternoon in the celebrated greenhouse of John Hovey" and that he "was also painfully extravagant in collecting plants for the window of my room." It would appear, first, that Farr has mixed up Charles Hovey with his nephew John; for Charles, as indicated above was the "celebrated" Hovey, and was known to be open and available to visitors. Of course, Farr may well have spent time with John, who was known to have had an interest in peonies. And then, more significantly, it would also appear that Farr collected much more than plants for his window during

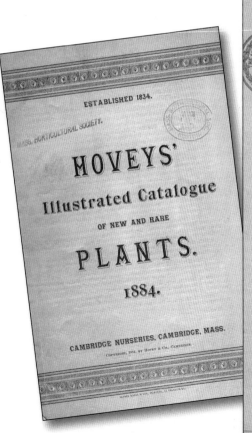

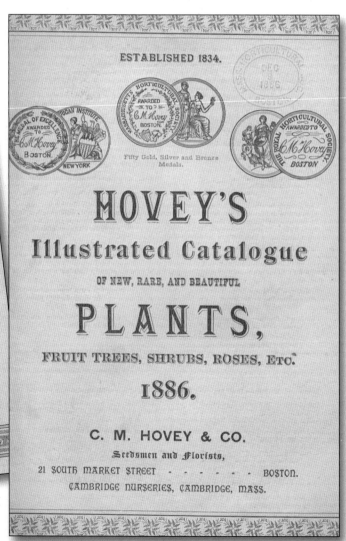

TO OUR FRIENDS AND PURCHASERS.

It is with unusual pleasure we now present our annual Catalogue for 1884, — the FIFTIETH YEAR, — and we believe we can claim a pretty long experience in the culture and dissemination of Trees, Shrubs, Plants, Flowers and Seeds of all kinds, and in the origination of numerous valuable varieties, now among the most popular and beautiful in cultivation. The hundreds of prizes and numerous silver medals awarded to us, both at home and abroad, are the best evidence of our endeavors to introduce only the very finest and most meritorious productions. Our Mr. C. M. Hovey, so long the editor of the *Magazine of Horticulture*, is too well known to render it necessary to offer additional evidence of the advantages we possess in estimating the comparative value of all new plants, shrubs or fruits, and the merits which entitle them to general cultivation.

Orders for Plants and Seeds. — We send plants or seeds either by mail or express, but we do not advise sending plants by mail only where there is no express office. We can send much larger, better, and stronger plants by express, which are sure to give satisfaction, and we add enough gratis to pay the express charges. Purchasers will find it for their interest to leave the selection to us, as it is often difficult to judge of the merit of varieties by descriptions.

Packing. — No charge is made for boxes, baskets, or packages (except in extra large specimens), and all packages are delivered in Boston free of charge. Our mode of packing is such that we can forward plants safely at all seasons of the year, without regard to cold or heat.

Our Gardens in Cambridge are within twenty-five minutes' time by horse cars from Scollay Square, Boston. Gentlemen wishing to see or consult Mr. C. M. Hovey personally, will find him at the nurseries until 12 M., and at office, No. 69 TREMONT STREET, Boston, from 1 till 3 P. M.

Plants and Seeds. — As our business includes both seeds and plants, as well as fruit and ornamental trees, shrubs, vines, etc., orders for both may be sent together, and additional express charges saved.

The Safe Arrival of Plants, seeds or bulbs by mail or express in good condition we guarantee. All complaints, however, should be made immediately on the receipt of the packages. Plants or seeds by freight are at the risk of the purchaser.

How to Send Money. — Remittances may be made either by Draft, Post-office Order, or Registered Letter. But in no case should bills be sent in a letter unless registered. Stamps may be sent when the amount is less than one dollar.

Name and Address. — Don't forget to give your Post-office address and State, distinctly written.

In order to prevent any delay and miscarriage of letters, our friends and correspondents are requested to

ADDRESS IN FULL,

HOVEY & CO. - - Cambridge Nurseries,
CAMBRIDGE, MASS.
TELEPHONE No. 7009.

Orders will also be received at

69 TREMONT STREET, and
16 SOUTH MARKET STREET, BOSTON, MASS.

INDEX.

his stay in Boston. We are never likely to know what Farr absorbed, but given this rich horticultural environment in Cambridge (and possibly also in nearby Jamaica Plain at the famous Arnold Arboretum), he probably learned a lot about nursery management, hybridizing, sources and varieties of plants and, in general, gained a base of knowledge and a charge of inspiration that would serve him well in Wyomissing.

*I*n 1885 Farr returned to Iowa, perhaps discouraged about not being the "musical prodigy" he had thought he was when he left in 1883. In Webster City, according to several biographical accounts, he established "a music business." The current reference librarian in Webster City, who has turned up a number of useful references to Farr in her data base, found only one music-business reference for Farr – a brief listing in the *Webster City and Hamilton County Directory* for 1886. Under the heading of "Music and Musical Instruments," appears "Farr, B.H., Second street." In Farr's own brief autobiography, he says nothing about his work there.

Instead, he reports that in Webster City he met "the lady who later became my wife" and, curiously, reveals that she had been at the Conservatory in Boston at the same time as he and "had studied at the same school under the same teachers and shared the same experiences although it was not until my return to Iowa that I met her." Anna Willis (1863-1940), a music teacher, was also the organist in the local Congregational church where he was choir leader. Near misses must have been even more frequent earlier because one biographical sketch on Bertrand Farr states that Anna Willis was born in West Mills, near Farmington, Maine, but that her "family had removed [to Webster City, Iowa] when she was a small child." And Bertrand and Anna were the same age.

Now Farr's life story continues to have some unclear reporting, but brings us near the point described in the first part of the first chapter. Farr says that after three years, now 1888, he "always loved Boston" and "went back to visit." Other accounts, including his obituary in the Farr Nursery "Special Memorial Issue," say he returned "to complete his education." In any case, his stay in Boston appears to have been short; for he was offered a position in Philadelphia variously reported as in a "music school" or a "music house." Farr's sister, in a 1964 letter, wrote that Bert had worked in Philadelphia "as an apprentice piano tuner in a piano factory." He writes that he "spent five [*sic*] very happy years in Philadelphia; but that, since his firm went out of business and he had had duties in Reading, he decided to settle there. The Reading business directory would seem to correct Farr's memory since it lists him as a piano tuner in Reading in 1891 – and beyond until 1904, when, as mentioned before, he went into a partnership to run a music store in Reading.

In early September of 1896, the newspapers in Webster City, Iowa reported that marriage licenses had been issued to Bertrand H. Farr, 32, and to Anna F. Willis, 32; and that invitations had been issued to their wedding in Webster City. The newspaper report of the wedding began, "The commodious home of Mr. and Mrs. C.E. Younkee, on west First street, was the scene of one of the most delightful and dainty wedding celebrations of the season, on Wednesday evening, Sept. 9th." The Rev. C.P. Boardman of the Congregational church performed the ceremony for the couple in view of the 40 guests. Anna wore "a beautiful costume of lavender and white lace and carried a large bouquet of white roses." Bertrand wore "a handsome and perfectly fitting full dress suit of conventional black." Mrs. Oppenheimer provided "sweet strains of music" on the piano. Later, "a dainty wedding supper was served, tissue covered shingles being used instead of tables." The article also reported that the newlyweds "were the recipients of many costly and beautiful presents, among them being a check for $500 from the parents of the groom." Then, "At 10:52 the happy couple, accompanied by Mr. and Mrs. W.H. Antes, left for Evansville, Wis., where they will remain several days at the latter's home."

View of Wyomissing Boulevard, ca. 1900, looking south from Penn Avenue, with Farr residence, the middle house

April 2007 view of house Farr built in 1896-97 at 118 Wyomissing Boulevard

Finally, the paper reports that the newlyweds "will reside at Reading, Penn., where an elegant new home is in course of construction." This "new home" in Wyomissing – the suburb of Reading just being developed – and his new life with his bride Anna were together leading to his new career as a horticulturist.

At the same time that he was collecting and growing all those plants that he would be offering in his first catalog, he was attending to other matters. His partnership with Howard E. Gerhardt in their store at 809 Penn Street in Reading, handling "pianos, organs, and musical merchandise," must have taken some of his time, and, one would guess, more than a little because in 1909 Farr bought the business from his partner and continued to own what became Farr's Music House at 809 Penn Street and then 643 Penn Street until 1912. As the developing suburb of Wyomissing was gaining buyers of lots and new residents, prominent people in the town such as Farr began to make plans to have Wyomissing become an incorporated borough. Borough status would give Wyomissing independence from its dependent political position within Spring Township and then the power to take charge of its schools, streets, other municipal facilities and finances. Early after 1900 Farr was part of a small group of men in Wyomissing planning their application and their strategy for incorporation, and in 1905 he was an important participant in a deposition held in Reading to defend the application. By 1905 Wyomissing had around 350 inhabitants, in 1906 it became incorporated as a borough, and Farr was elected chief burgess. This mostly ceremonial position probably did not take much of Farr's time, but still meant another set of distractions from his beloved plants. In the 1910 census he now listed himself as "farmer" with a "nursery"; Anna Farr listed herself as "music teacher." The Farrs never had children, but during this early time in their marriage Bertrand's brother Edward, ten years younger, was also working in Reading as a piano tuner and lived with the Farrs from their beginning in Wyomissing until 1914. Still, Farr took time to write a poem:

View of Wyomissing Boulevard, ca. early 1900's, looking north, with Farr residence second on left and "The Circle" in foreground

WHEN CARRIE CLEANS THE ROOM

On days when inspiration lags
  And I go out to walk
Among the fields of purple flags
  To woo the elusive thought
Straightway, amuck, with might and vim
  Raising the dust with an awful din
With broom and brush, and a method grim
  Then Carrie cleans the room.

When I return all unsuspecting
  To gaze upon the scene dejecting
Spick and span; stiff and prim;
  A transformation weird, uncanny
Things have vanished out of sight
  Hid in every nook and cranny;
From desk to dresser and closet-door
  There is not a damn thing on the floor;
Empty! spooky! like I'd croaked.
  You would ne'er believe I lived there.
FOR CARRIE CLEANED THE ROOM.

—Bertrand H. Farr, June 1908

"The composition of a first catalogue under trying conditions."

Before Carrie emptied Farr's room, he, of course, had been filling up for the past several years the vacant fields in Wyomissing and nearby with his thousands of plants, with his catalog offerings of 1,667 cultivars. Having launched that first catalog in 1908 for the season of 1909, Farr was ready to expand his nursery business; and a key feature was The Iris.

Chapter 3

The Iris

There is a peculiar charm about the Iris that appeals irresistibly to those whose taste for the refined and the delicately beautiful leads them to seek a close acquaintance with it. The rare and ethereal beauty of its soft, iridescent coloring, and its frail, orchid-like formation, is likely to pass unnoticed by the careless observer....

But to him who stops to gaze into the depths of the Iris flower, and comes under the magic spell, a new world is opened. For an Iris garden is a floral world unto itself; and an Iris enthusiast may have full scope for his wildest fancies....

Irises are a leading specialty with us, and our collection of several hundred varieties contains many new and rare ones not to be found elsewhere. They have been thoroughly tested and can be relied upon as being distinct and true to name.

—Bertrand H. Farr
Catalog, First Edition, 1908

Dramatic as Farr's whole 1908 catalog was – springing up out of practically nowhere from a "music man" and offering a vast array of plants – it really was the catalog's very first section devoted to The Iris that created a momentous event in America's horticultural world. Irisarian contemporaries of Farr's as well as modern iris experts have written about Farr's remarkable achievements stemming from this first catalog and just beyond. John C. Wister (1887-1982), a founding member in 1920 of the American Iris Society and its first president, dedicated his 1927 book on the iris "To the memory of Bertrand H. Farr, who more than any other man made the present popularity of the iris in America possible." In his chapter on modern iris history, Wister emphasizes that "it was really not until the new century that the real pioneer of American Iris began his work in Wyomissing, Pennsylvania." Supporting this claim three years earlier, Wister wrote, "[Farr] was the first person to import a collection of modern improved varieties, and the first to place these before the American gardening public. He was also the first American to breed and introduce new varieties...."

R.S. Sturtevant (1889-1955), the Society's first secretary, wrote in 1925 about one of Farr's first introductions in 1909: "Juniata has probably been used more than any other American variety as a parent..." Clarence Mahan, a more recent president of the American Iris Society, wrote in 2007, "'Juniata' was a standout in the garden from the time of its introduction because its flower stalks towered above all others, often exceeding four feet...." "Other hybridizers incorporated 'Juniata' into their breeding programs. As a parent of new, improved irises, it was probably Farr's most important iris."

Mahan goes on to mention other important Farr "firsts," explaining that all of

From 1911 catalog with Farr's caption: *Farr's new Iris "Juniata."*
This shows the graceful fountain-like effect of the foliage and relative height.
The tallest variety in my collection.

Farr's earliest irises were *diploids*, irises with two sets of chromosomes; however, in 1912 he hybridized and introduced 'Tromagnifica' and 'Trosuperba,' both *tetraploids* with four sets of chromosomes, "the first two tetraploid irises bred and introduced by an American hybridizer." Mahan then adds, "Most of the 'red' irises in our gardens today are descended from 'Trosuperba.'"

Farr created not only these "firsts" but also the "mosts." As Mahan writes, "All the time [Farr] was adding new plants to his collection he was working toward opening a plant nursery. … His first catalogue contained the most extensive lists of iris and peony cultivars offered to American gardeners up to that time." And it was the *bearded* iris that was so significant: "The bearded iris was not one of America's favorite garden plants in the 19th century." "Farr taught Americans to appreciate the beauty and merits of the bearded iris."

To underscore from another angle Farr's pioneering work, Mahan emphasizes that "When Farr began breeding irises there was no iris society, no standard to use in determining merits of seedlings, no understanding of iris genetics, and no instructional manual. And yet all of Farr's early iris introductions were distinctive."

Finally, coming up with the key words for all these tributes to Farr, two iris writers, in 1954, state, "It is *astonishing* [italics mine] the success Mr. Farr had in producing a fine batch of varieties in a *short space of time* [italics mine], especially considering that he had no iris experience, and no parentage record of the varieties used in making crosses." Indeed, the whole catalog was astonishing on considering these iris introductions, the total number of plants and Farr's accomplishing all this without any formal training in just ten years' time.

*A*fter that first "distinctive" set of iris introductions praised by Mahan, Farr continued hybridizing and offering more of his iris cultivars. As printed in his catalogs, here is the record of these irises. Because some irises, for example **Quaker Lady**, may have been available in a year different from the catalog year, they might be listed differently on the American Iris Society checklist:

First Edition, 1908: **Glory of Reading, Iroquois, Juniata, Leda, Montezuma, Mt. Penn, Windham** and **Wyomissing.**

Second Edition, 1909-10: **Rose Unique** and **Tecumseh.**

Fourth Edition, 1912-13: **Aletha, Anna Farr, Aurora, Blue Jay, Chester Hunt, Eldorado** (later changed to **Minnehaha**), **Erich, Hiawatha, Hugo, Lewis Trowbridge, Mary Garden, Mary Gray, Navajo, Oriental, Quaker Lady*** and **Red Cloud.** (***Quaker Lady** is listed as 1909 by the American Iris Society checklist.)

Fifth Edition, 1915: **E.L. Crandall, Nokomis, Pocahontas** and **Powhatan.**

Sixth Edition, 1916-17: **James Boyd, Massasoit** and **Shrewsbury.**

Seventh Edition, 1920-21: **Brandywine, Georgia, Mary Orth** and **Seminole.** Also, **Paxatawney** and **Swatara** were included though the American Iris Society lists them as 1918's.

(After 1921 Farr switched to smaller catalogs.)

1923: **Cecile Minturn, Sea-Gull** and **Japanesque.**

1924: **Catalosa, Inca** and **Mildred Presby.**

Several more of his irises Farr offered but, for some reason, did not identify as his:

1909: **Jean Ribaud**

1912: **Grandis, Lucy, Lutea Maculata, Mrs. Tait, Pallida Perfecta, Trocelestial, Tromagnifica** and **Trosuperba.**

After Farr's death in 1924, irises he had hybridized were offered by the succeeding Farr Nursery:

1926: **Apache** and **Cattleya.**

1930: **Conestoga.**

There were also a few other bearded iris cultivars that Farr hybridized and named but were not really offered for sale or registered. As the above lists document, however, one can safely say that Farr presented to the American public at least 57 new irises.

Farr's astonishing achievements of introducing this many new irises of his own and also of having the largest collection of irises in the country depended on two related activities – importing irises and then using some of them for hybridizing. About the latter activity, Farr wrote in 1915, "During recent years I have found the hybridizing and raising of seedling Irises a very interesting *pastime* [italics mine]. Of the many thousands raised, scarcely any two are exactly alike. From the many fine forms, I have selected the following [and 30 of his irises up to this 1915 time do follow] which I consider to be the very best." The amount of time and work it takes for "hybridizing and raising," as will be described

Farr's iris field and his caption from 1911 catalog: *June ushers in the great Germanica family – the bearded Irises with their broad mass of color – the true Fleur-de-lis.*

shortly, should make one wonder about Farr's use of "pastime." But his use does suggest a common theme with some nurserymen – a blurring of hobby and business. Another blurring occurred in Farr's case, what could be called a "scientific blurring," in that Farr apparently did not keep parentage records of his hybrids. One good reason for this omission is that in the early years of his nursery, according to one knowledgeable source, he depended on bees to do the hybridizing and only later used the more controlled method described below.

About Farr's process of importing and collecting irises, there seems to be almost nothing written from Farr; but there is some information from later sources. A botanical journal from 1953 asserts that Farr "purchased his first great collection totaling several hundred varieties divided into six so-called botanical sections" from Peter Barr's nursery in England. Barr & Sons was one of many famous 19th century European nurseries that were successfully expanding the variety and quality of many kinds of plants and adding to horticultural knowledge. The "six so-called botanical sections" above refers to the six color-and-pattern categories (not really botanical names despite their Latinate form), which Peter Barr devised as shorthand descriptions of bearded irises and which Farr led the way in America to employing while importing Barr's irises. Barr & Sons had its main office and store in Covent Garden, London and its nursery at Ditton Hill, Surbiton, Surrey. In its 1901 catalog the nursery asserted that it offered a collection of bearded irises "the most complete in Europe" and listed 315 iris varieties.

Mahan adds that in addition to Barr & Sons, "Farr imported every iris cultivar he could obtain from various French nurseries…." The likely ones include Vilmorin-Andrieux & Cie in Paris, including the collection of Eugene Verdier, which the Parisian company bought out after his death in 1902, and Ferdinand Cayeux. Another European grower that Mahan cites and also is clearly identified in Farr's 1911 catalog is Goos & Koenemann, a famous German nursery in Nieder-Walluf, between Wiesbaden and Ruedesheim on the Rhine River. Otherwise, Farr's catalogs did not identify the sources of his imported irises until 1922.

With his large collection of irises from England, France, and Germany and maybe some from America as well, he had plenty of irises to choose from to exercise his pastime of hybridizing and raising his own new cultivars.

Iris Sibirica orientalis. A sea of ultramarine blue.
From 1911 catalog.

Iris Kempferi, the crowning glory of all, arrayed in richest blue, and purple, and gold.

Herbst 1895.

Frühjahr 1896.

Hoflieferanten Sr. Königlichen Hoheit
des Grossherzogs von Hessen.

MASS. HORTICULTURAL SOCIETY.

GOOS & KOENEMANN

NIEDER-WALLUF

(RHEINGAU).

Eulalia japonica gracillima univittata
Siehe Seite 37.

Fall 1895, Spring 1896 catalog cover from a nursery that supplied Farr with irises

The first steps in hybridizing bearded irises, by hand rather than by bees, are fairly simple and easy. The basic process involves transferring the pollen from the anther of one iris to the stigmatic lip of another iris so that the pollen parent is crossed with the seed parent, which later in the season produces a pod of seeds, which, of course, can later be planted to produce new irises.

Fortunately, one of Farr's employees has provided a detailed account of Farr's methods. John Ravel began work with Farr in 1913 "as a general nursery worker and worked his way up to supervisor of all iris activities." He is quoted in a 1929 American Iris Society article as stating that he "pollenized, observed, noted, trued, discarded, transplanted and handled millions of iris" during the 11 years he worked until Farr's death and then five more years beyond.

Farr did the hybridizing himself, assisted by John and another employee, by selecting plants of just *one* iris cultivar as pollen parents and then crossing them with as many as 100 different seed parents ("Farr believed in quantity and haphazard crosses," Ravel writes.) The seeds from each of the resulting 100 different sets of seed pods "were collected, dried, and planted one pod to a flat." Left outdoors so that the frost later on would crack their shells, the seeds were taken indoors for the winter and by early spring would have sprouted and then be ready for replanting outdoors.

The next year these plants would have some blooms, but not enough for judging them. The process of observing and selecting Farr would do the following spring, by now the fourth year in this sequence. The plants "that met Mr. Farr's interest were moved to the 'selected seedlings' bed. Out of this bed, not more than one of one hundred were eventually introduced. In all, not more than one out of five thousand of the original seedlings ever got to be introduced." And then, really to emphasize the enormous ratio of effort to product, "Many times a new variety was propagated to the extent of several thousand plants and then discarded…because something better came along." Ravel does not fully cover the whole process leading to a sufficient number of plants of a given "star" cultivar to market in a catalog, but in Farr's era and geographical location the time from crossing plants to the time of plant sufficiency would have been seven to nine years and involved thousands of plants never used.

Given this kind of "production" process – one that probably was even more difficult for Farr when he started years earlier than Ravel's employment with who-knows-what kind of nursery help – one can appreciate anew the effort and the passion and, what must have been, the joy all these irises meant to him. Unfortunately, the photographs of him with his irises and other plants portray him as an unsmiling, even somber, gentleman.

However, fellow irisarians like Frank Presby, treasurer-to-be of the American Iris Society, write about spending the day in Wyomissing with Farr walking the fields and helping to name the new hybrid irises and about Farr's frequent return visits with Presby in New York and their "talking over flowers in general." Or John Wister's statement that "It was always a joy to go around with Mr. Farr because he was always interested in all the plants as plants…." also suggests both enthusiasm and collegiality. We also have his written words to overcome any misimpression of his lack of emotion. And, again, it takes the form of a poem from his Seventh Catalog of 1920:

Iris Flower, what can you tell
Of the mysteries that dwell
In the opal depths of your fragile shell?

Is it some Fairy whose wand has spun
Those gossamer threads with dewdrops hung,
Reflecting the glow of the morning sun?

Or is it a Spirit that dwells within,
With a message from Heaven to mortal men
Of hope and promise at the rainbow's end?

Iris Flower, you speak to me
Of fair and wondrous worlds that be
In the azure depths of Infinity.

Fair messenger from out of the great
Unknown,
I yield to the touch of your magic wand,
And dream and dream with you alone.

Far away, through Heaven's azure blue,
We float on misty clouds of dew
Through ever-changing scenes, and
delights forever new.

There's a gleam of the gold of Ophir
Through the purple robes of Night.
There's a glint of the Frost King's
palace
Aglow with Aurora's light.

Iris Flower, to me you tell
All the mysteries that dwell
In the opal depths of your fragile shell.
—B.H.F.

Less mystical-poetical was Farr's success in San Francisco in 1915. From Wyomissing that year he shipped out about 1,500 iris plants to compete in the Panama-Pacific International Exposition. As Farr explained, he formed this entry from "the cream of standard varieties, the finest European novelties, and my own seedlings raised here at Wyomissing." In another account of Farr's San Francisco entry, an iris expert writes "he had the most modern and comprehensive garden of all the tall bearded irises...." Farr won the Gold Medal for the best collection and set off a chain reaction. John Wister wrote that Farr's collection "for the first time definitely placed American Irises on the map, and undoubtedly the publicity from that show encouraged many other breeders to follow his example." Two later writers stated, "The publicity from this exhibit was world wide and gave American interest in iris a real boost."

Bertrand Farr had come a long way to achieve this international fame, a way conditioned from the time back in his boyhood days in Iowa:

Horticultural Hall, Panama-Pacific International Exposition in San Francisco, 1915, where Farr won a Gold Medal

There was the clear, open water in the center, hedged around by the tall, green rushes, where the red-winged blackbirds had their nests. Farther out, surrounding it all with a halo of shimmering blue, like the heavens themselves, grew the Irises —water flags, we called them. You had to wade to get to them, and the blackbirds would do a deal of scolding; but outside, rising straight up from the tall meadow grass, the bobolink would burst forth into such a rapturous ecstasy of joyous song that you stood transfixed with wonder, and as you listened to the bird, and gazed into the depths of the fragile flower in your hand, reveling in its soft, delicate beauty, it seemed as if life was all joy, and beauty, and gentleness.

—*Bertrand H. Farr, Second Catalog, 1909-10*

Quaker Lady (Farr, 1909)

Juniata (Farr, 1909)

Wyomissing (Farr, 1909)

ALL PHOTOS: COURTESY OF MIKE LOWE

Offspring of pod parent Juniata, Conquistador (Mohr, 1923)

Anna Farr (Farr, 1913)

Apache (Farr, 1926)

Mary Orth (Farr, 1920)

Mildred Presby (Farr, 1924)

44

ALL PHOTOGRAPHS ON PAGES 44, 45, 46 & 48 ARE FROM GLASS SLIDES
MADE BY FARR'S PUBLISHER J. HORACE MCFARLAND CO.

Georgia (Farr, 1920)

Inca (Farr, 1922)

Montezuma (Farr, 1909)

Japanesque (Farr, 1922)

Farr's iris field ca. 1907.

Farr's New Seedling Irises, grown at Wyomissing

1. Blue Jay
2. Louis Trowbridge
3. Windham
4. Nokomis
5. Iroquois
6. Mary Garden
7. Mt. Penn
8. Mary Gray
9. Quaker Lady
10. Anna Farr
11. Navajo

Page from 1915 catalog

Marie Lemoine (Calot, 1869)

Marie Crousse (Crousse, 1892)

Souvenir de Maxine Cornu (Lemoine)

Kelway's Queen (Kelway)

Clockwise from above: Catharine Keiser Reed, as little girl, with *Elie Chevalier* (Dessert, 1908) in a section of Farr's Dream Garden. *Rosa Bonheur* (Dessert, 1905). Japanese tree peony, *shiro fugen*. Unidentified children in Farr's peony field with City of Reading and Mount Penn in background.

These beautiful Peonies were grown at Wyomissing. Photographed in June, 1914

1. Cavalleria Rusticana
2. Duchess of Teck
3. Marguerite Girard
4. M. Hyppolyte Dellille
5. Karl Rosenfield
6. Madame Moutot

Page from 1915 catalog.

Chapter 4

The Peony

BERTRAND H. FARR, PEONY WIZARD, MADE WYOMISSING WORLD RENOWNED

His garden mecca for horticulturists, now in midst of Glory

These are days of glory in the peony fields of Wyomissing, days of additional crowns upon the head of their master, that genius of hardy plants, Bertrand H. Farr. Farr peonies are known far and wide, and from as far as they are known come horticulturists to see them, even from Holland.

Acres and acres of white, pink, and red blooms, with their varicolored relatives transform the places between the tree-shaded boulevards into a paradise of scent and gorgeousness. To see them is to desire them, and the result is a continual procession of visitors, coming with hope, going with content.

—Reading Telegram, June 8, 1912

*I*n contrast to his work hybridizing and introducing irises, Bertrand Farr concentrated on collecting as many peonies as he could. Although he did spend some time hybridizing peonies – in 1916 and again in 1918 he entered seedling peonies named only No. 2 and No. 6 in the peony shows in Cleveland and Detroit – apparently no peonies of his were introduced in his catalogs. Another contrast will appear in the ways that Farr wrote about irises and peonies in his catalogs.

Among some of Farr's acquaintances there were differing opinions over whether his favorite plant was The Iris or The Peony. However, one of Farr's special friends from both the iris and the peony worlds neatly resolved the issue in this way: "I do not even know which of his two favorite flowers he loved best. I doubt if he could have answered that question himself. For as he was a wise and tolerant man in his human relations so, in his attitude towards the many vari-

1914 photo of Farr with peonies

eties of flowers with which he busied himself, he was always inclined rather to look for the good qualities than to pick on some defect by which he might condemn." This same friend also wrote about Bertrand Farr's major service to peony horticulture and to the initial purpose of the American Peony Society.

Arthur Percy Saunders (1869-1953), in the early 1900's was on his way to becoming a distinguished professor of chemistry at Hamilton College and, in parallel with Farr, was beginning to collect a large number of peonies at his home in Clinton, New York and later would become world-famous as a peony hybridizer. In 1928, having served as Secretary-Editor of the American Peony Society from 1911 to 1923, he wrote a history of the Society, in which Farr played a prominent part and gained much knowledge of peonies and many friends along the way.

In 1902 Charles W. Ward, owner of the Cottage Gardens Nursery on Long Island, wrote a letter to a number of other American peony growers suggesting they form an association "for the purpose of advancing the public interest in the peony, and especially straightening out peony nomenclature." The letter succeeded so well that by 1903 the Society was organized with 37 nurserymen members and by 1904 was incorporated. As Saunders then writes, the main purpose of the Society initially was "not to hold meetings nor to stage exhibitions," but rather "to attack the difficult question of peony nomenclature and to bring order out of the confusion which then reigned among the named peonies in commerce." The same peony was often sold under a variety of different names, and many different peonies were often sold under just one name.

To begin to overcome these problems, two sets of appeals went out, first to M. August Dessert in Chenonceaux, France "to compile a descriptive list of varieties introduced by Belgian and French growers" (Dessert being one of the famous sources of peonies for Farr) and to Society members to compile a list of their varieties from several American growers, from Kelway & Sons in England, and from Japanese sources, altogether producing a master list of around 1,000 varieties, but only a *printed* list.

From Farr's 1915 catalog: *A portion of one of the fields of Peonies at Wyomissing in June, 1914.*

The second set of appeals was sent in August 1904 to the important peony growers in Europe and America to voluntarily send to Cornell University actual specimens of all their peony varieties so that they could be assembled and planted there and then studied and compared in order to eliminate duplicates, establish the correct names, and write accurate descriptions of the established varieties. In A.P. Saunders' history, he identifies the names of all the nurserymen who responded along with the number of peonies sent. Eight European growers sent a total of 871 plants, and 22 American growers sent 1,818. Later contributions swelled the total to well over 3,000 plants.

Interestingly, B.H. Farr, responding with 147 peonies to this 1904 appeal, sent the sixth largest number of peonies from among the 30 growers, the third largest among the Americans. In an unpublished essay, Farr wrote that since the time he had acquired his first peony (and not a real, modern one) from his aunt for bringing in her cow, he had not owned another peony for 25 years, i.e., up to the time when he moved to Wyomissing. He writes:

[W]hen in 1897 I came to Wyomissing, where I could have a small garden, one of the first things I determined was to have a complete collection of Peonies, 'a white one, a red one, and a pink one.' Then I discovered that Ellwanger & Barry [Rochester, N.Y.] had a grand collection as many as twenty kinds. After I had these, one of Lemoine's [Nancy, France] catalogues fell into my hands and, after some hesitation over the extravagance, I made the plunge. I sent to him my first foreign order in 1901. Only then did I realize what was before me, but it was too late. The Peony bug had gotten me, as it had many others, and will get you too if it once gets fairly hold of you. Orders from Dessert and others soon followed. Then from Kelway in England.

Photo from 1911 catalog with unidentified woman, but presumed to be Anna Farr

Therefore, in just a few years Farr had collected at least 147 different peonies, and somehow had become known as a grower although he was not yet a member of the Society and wrote that he was "not then in touch with these people." But he had heard of the Society; and about the Society's annual meeting in 1906 Farr writes, "I came home, packed my grip and started to Boston to see the Peony Show, and learn something about Peonies. At this show I got my first real inspiration."

From that inspiring experience in Boston – and how appropriate in his beloved Boston, the scene of his earlier days at Hovey & Co. and the Conservatory of Music – it was to be a rapid rise in the peony world for Bertrand Farr.

Saunders explains that someone special had to be found to carry out this daunting project of comparison and identification. "Cornell University had supplied a very competent young man, Mr. J. Eliot Coit [who was to gain his Ph. D from Cornell in 1907] to take care of the work on the spot, but there was needed a thoroughly equipped expert, one familiar with peonies by long experience, who would be willing to sacrifice his time and his own business interests during the height of the [growing] season for the sake of accomplishing the great task...." Quite surprisingly, Farr agreed and was given "the main burden of the undertaking." It is surprising

54

Kelway's Pæonies

CAPTIVATE THE WORLD

M. Williams

HARDY HERBACEOUS PERENNIAL.

The Pæony is the Fashionable Flower. Kelway & Son made it so with **their improved varieties.**

Planting season :

Autumn, favourable weather in winter, and spring.

Flowering season :

May and June.

The Fashionable Flower.

Copyright, K. & S.

Beauty and Suitability. Herbaceous *Pæonies* are the most beautiful, the noblest and the grandest of all Hardy Perennial Plants, and should be in every garden, large or small ; in beds, borders, shrubberies, or drives ; in park, grass walk, or woodland. They should be planted in masses for distant colour effect, in lines straight or curving on the margin of shrubberies, and in groups between shrubs ; in large and small beds in the midst of turf ; in borders at the foot of walls, and in mixed borders at constant intervals ; they should, in their less expensive kinds, be planted freely in copses, woods, and the rougher parts of the garden ; all these situations they adorn.

It is worthy of note that while *Pæonies* vie with the Rhododendron in the showy character of their blooms, they have this advantage over the latter, that they do not require peat or loam for their culture.

Hardiness. Whether in the old kinds or in KELWAY's lovely new varieties, they will thrive in practically any position, and there is hardly one in which they will not flourish to perfection ; they are amenable to the simplest treatment in any soil, and are as hardy as the dock by the wayside ; they need not the slightest protection, as neither the severest frost nor the most biting wind does them hurt.

because Farr had just barely arrived on the scene in 1906 in Boston and, by comparison with other Society members, was not a grower with "long experience." Nevertheless, Farr was willing to take time from his music store and nursery; and because he must have been deemed sufficiently experienced with peonies for the task and have earned the trust of the Society leadership, he gained the head job.

This trust must have come partly from his eager participation in the Boston meeting and from what many have described as his genial manner. Farr writes about his enthusiasm over meeting many Society members and about visiting local members and their nearby nurseries. Apparently on his own he went to the Boston suburbs to visit T.C. Thurlow "at his delightful and hospitable home" in West Newbury. He visited "James McKissock and his beautiful collection at West Newton." And "Up at Wellesley Hills [he] found Mr. [E.J.] Shaylor among his peonies."

Farr did have important help from Joseph Dauphin, an expert in European peonies from the Cottage Gardens Nursery, and from two Cornell men, Coit and Leon D. Batchelor, who published the group's results in a series of Cornell Bulletins. Starting in 1907, Farr met with the group, as he reports, for parts of six successive Junes; and, as Saunders reports, they met at Cornell and also at Cottage Gardens on Long Island and at Wyomissing. Saunders cites one clear example of the confusion this Nomenclature Committee had to confront: "Edulis Superba was found to have been sent to Cornell under twenty-three different names, sometimes even under three or four different names from the same nursery! Indeed, almost all widely grown varieties existed in the trade under more than one name."

For Farr's work on the compressing, ordering, and describing of peony cultivars, Saunders states, "Mr. Farr often expressed himself as well satisfied with what he had gained in return for his labor; and he was recognized from that time on to his death, in 1924, as the leading peony authority in this country, or indeed in any country." Impossible to measure, of course, but Farr's labor with so many peony plants and in collaboration with the Cornell botanists must have taught him much to earn this accolade.

In 1909 Charles Ward, the man who had initiated the process leading to the Society's founding and had been serving as its first president since 1903, resigned for health reasons. Bertrand Farr then became president, serving until 1916 and then remaining as a director until his death. Saunders pays tribute to Charles Ward and to Arthur Fewkes, the long-serving secretary from 1903 to 1911, for their combined leadership in the formative years of the Soci-

1908-9
Greetings

To our Friends and Patrons:

WE present with pleasure the most complete and comprehensive Catalogue of Peonies ever published in this country. The ever increasing demand for this Queen of Spring flower has compelled us to increase our stock and we now have some ten acres of land devoted exclusively to the culture of the Peony. Many of the varieties listed herein are offered by us for the first time and, with some varieties, the stock is so limited that we are compelled to restrict the quantity that will be sold to any one customer.

We have spared no expense in adding to our collection of illustrations in order that our friends and patrons may be more fully informed as to the character of the newer and rarer varieties. These illustrations are faithful reproductions of photographs made of the blooms grown on our premises. The extensive field notes which are taken each year enable us to add materially to the descriptive matter, our aim being to give only authentic descriptions that will convey to intending purchasers a clear idea of the variety so far as this can possibly be done.

OUR STOCK
Size of Plants Shipped

It has been our custom during past years to list the sizes under divisions and one, two and three year roots. This year we will send out one and two year old roots only. In order to inform our patrons more fully as regards the quality of the stock they may expect to receive, we have had a photograph taken of samples of these roots—both one and two year old—a reproduction of which appears on page three of this Catalogue.

OUR PRICES

Remember that our prices are for strong roots, one and two years established, which are far superior to the divisions frequently offered. These established roots are surer to grow and will make strong blooming plants one to two years sooner than the divisions. The fact that established roots give our customers better satisfaction, coupled with our large increase of stock, has decided us to abandon supplying divisions and to hereafter furnish established plants only.

We take this opportunity of thanking our friends and patrons for their kind support and can assure them that it will be our endeavor to fill all orders with that high grade of stock which will secure for us a continuance of their patronage.

COTTAGE GARDENS NURSERY COMPANY, Inc.
QUEENS, N. Y.

ety and then concludes, "But with these two, Mr. Ward and Mr. Fewkes, must always be remembered Mr. Farr, who did more than anyone else, perhaps, to make the peony known and appreciated by the gardening public in this country."

At the Society's annual meetings each year competitive peony shows were a major reason for the events, and Farr won three First Prizes and many Gold Medals for his collections of peonies in 1909, 1914, 1916, 1918, and 1919 in Long Island, Chicago, New York, Cleveland, and Detroit respectively. What may well have been an even more rewarding experience for him, however, was his chance to be the home nurseryman at the annual meeting held on June 10-11, 1920 at The Berkshire Hotel in Reading.

Farr, serving as one of the judges and not competing in the exhibition, provided several thousand of his peonies to supplement the already bursting array of cut-flower displays on the hotel's main floor. The *Reading Eagle,* supporting the hometown man, reported that "Mr. Farr's exhibit was by far the largest and in many respects the most handsome of the show," one that "would have swept away many prizes from the visiting nurserymen" had he chosen to compete. The *Eagle* emphasized that express shipments of peonies had been arriving in Reading from more than a dozen states around the country and from Canada, filling up the lobby and spilling into the grill of The Berkshire and beyond. "Not only are the flowers in evidence [in the hotel], but in every part of Reading. The civic division of the Woman's Club…arranged beautiful displays in store windows and in public places in all parts of the city. This in reality is peony week in Reading." Beyond all these cut peonies, the *Reading News-Times* reported this opportunity to see Farr's live peonies: "For the delegates attending, there is a free service to Farr's peony farm and as early as 4:30 Friday morning many visitors were there. The peonies are at their best at the break of day and many went to see them open for the day."

The Secretary of the Peony Society, in his later report on the meeting in Reading, was initially less enthusiastic than the local news reporters. He complained about the lack of natural light for the peony displays (admittedly, an annual complaint), but did reveal a sense of humor: the light for the amateur classes was "the sort of light in which you could not tell an oyster from an asparagus tip." He also wished that there had been more exhibitors in the "open classes," but then went on to report the results of the competition in the total of 41 different classes. Of special local interest was the second place prize going in the amateur class for a vase of three blooms in light pink to Mrs. Sylvester Keyser [sic] of Wyomissing, the mother of Farr's stableman and the grandmother of Catharine Keiser Reed. Catharine has stated that her grandmother had found the peonies growing in her mulch pile and, on a lark, entered them in the competition under Farr's urging.

The Society Secretary, now more positive, expressed gratitude to Farr for staging "a fine lot of blooms and a lot of fine blooms," for his large vases with 25 to 50 blooms and his smaller ones with three to six. Especially appealing to the Secretary's critical eye were Farr's "astonishing bunch of Duke of Wellington" and a lovely vase of Marie Jacquin. Finally, "the best thing about this show was not the show itself, but the opportunity it gave to our members to visit the peony and iris fields at Wyomissing," facilities for which "were generously afforded by the Chamber of Commerce and Mr. Farr himself."

The formation of the American Peony Society in 1903 had given Bertrand Farr an important institutional framework for his life as a peony man – his friendships with many other grower-members, his work on the Nomenclature Committee, his presidency, and here in Reading in 1920 a role as the "Prince of Peonies."

*I*n writing about the peony in his 1911 catalog essay, Farr makes a comparison between the way the iris and the peony affect the beholder – the difference between the dreaming and the beyond that would set you apart versus the immediate sense experiences that would hold you to the present and your common humanity:

The iridescent beauty of the iris makes you a dreamer of far-away things, that of the Peony awakens you to the joy of life and the glory of June. Rich with the warmth of its glowing colors, intoxicating in its delicious fragrance, its great, big, flowers make a universal appeal to human interest.

Published in 1929, after Farr's death, in the Peony Society's *Bulletin*, is a poem to the peony by a writer identified only as "a Fan," but offered in the Society's index as written by Farr and presumably found and sent in after Farr died. The poem's message certainly echoes the prose version above, even as the peony becomes personified as a charming woman:

Oh Peony! Throw Out Your Charms
By a Fan

Oh peony! to others throw out your charms,
    Tell them the truths you yearly tell to me;
Show them your beauty as each soul it warms,
    Throw out to them your lure, your symmetry,
Let them behold your beauty with clear eye;
    Your form, carriage, your grace and dignity.
By your sweet fragrance charm each one now nigh
    That your beauty may fill each heart with glee.
Disclose not all the secrets that you know,
    Sing out your mystic song; each soul appease.
Speak nature's tongue to all where 'ere you grow,
    That minds may be tranquil and souls at ease.
Convey to all what you convey to me,
    That they speak beauty everlastingly.

However, in writing about the peony, Farr was usually much more prosaic, focusing on the early history of the peony, its cultivation in Europe, the work of some American growers, and his time at Cornell with the nomenclature project.

Farr briefly touches on the Tree Peony in China as being its "chief pride and glory for 1,400 years, a theme of their poets and painters, and prized by their emperors for the beauty and fragrance of their flowers…." He then jumps to the modern European Peony, "descended from *Paeonia albiflora*, a native of Siberia," i.e, the herbaceous Peony, which differs from the Tree Peony in having a non-woody stem which dies back to the ground in the fall. Farr relates how the European cultivated peony had an aristocratic birth through "M. Jacques, gardener to King Louis Phillipe," and through three amateur French gardeners who imported "the best varieties from China and Japan" around 1850. Victor Verdier inherited the king's collection from his uncle M. Jacques. From the amateur Comte de Cussy, Jacques Calot inherited his collection, raising peonies until 1872, and then passing the collection to Felix Crousse, who marketed both Calot's and his own varieties until 1889. Farr rates these Calot-Crousse peonies as "raising the standards of excellence to a height that has never been surpassed, unless it be by the splendid varieties in recent years by that greatest of all the world's hybridizers, Victor Lemoine, whose establishment at Nancy is the place formerly occupied by Crousse." In addition to this succession of all-French growers, Farr then mentions Etienne Mechin, another amateur active at the same time as Calot and Crousse, who was succeeded by his grandson Auguste Dessert, "considered today [1915] the greatest living authority on Peonies" and introducing "some of the most beautiful additions" to the varieties already grown by the above French specialists.

Continuing his brief essay on famous peony growers who are represented with many varieties in his catalog, Farr mentions Kelway & Sons, the best peony nursery in England at the time, started by James Kelway in Langport, Somerset, and then assisted by his son William and grandson James. In America, Farr identifies John Richardson of Dorchester, Massachusetts, with his 18 strong varieties, which were not offered for sale until after his death in 1887. H.A. Terry, in Crescent, Iowa, right at the western border of the state, developed 51 varieties that Farr carried. About George H. Hollis, of South Weymouth, Massachusetts, Farr writes fondly that he first met him in Boston in 1906 and visited him at his home in 1910, the year before Hollis died. Hollis is represented with 17 peonies in Farr's catalog.

Altogether, in his 1915-16, Fifth Edition Catalog – with its categories of French, English, American, Japanese, Early Blooming, Single, and Tree Peonies – Farr lists a total of 566 different cultivars. About this collection he writes, " It has been my ambition to possess a complete collection of all distinct varieties of merit, and my catalog of Peonies, large as it is, contains, with but few exceptions, only varieties of known origin, all synonyms or duplicates having been eliminated. It is made up largely of the original productions of Lemoine, Dessert, Crousse and Calot, among which I have yet to see a really poor Peony."

Then in his next catalog, the Sixth for 1918, he announces, almost unobtrusively near the end of the peony section, "It is my great pleasure to be able to inform my patrons that I have become the fortunate possessor of the largest and most noted collection of Tree Peonies in France – that of Brochet & Sons, successors to the famous Paillet Nurseries, Chatenay – through the purchase of their entire stock of upwards of 5,000 plants in 238 varieties." With his over 800 varieties of peonies, Bertrand Farr has surely now succeeded in surrounding himself – and the Wyomissing community – with flowers beautiful and renowned.

Index to Peonies

Index to peony offerings in Farr's 1920 catalog

My Dream Garden which is coming to be a real garden, with Peonies and Irises in glorious abandon; with Deutzias, and Philadelphus, and Lilacs that make the air heavy with their fragrance

Page from 1920 catalog

Page from 1912 catalog: *Typical flowers of Lemoine's Double-Flowering Lilac*

Top left, *Ophir* (Farr, 1924), top right, *Bertrand H. Farr* (Stout, 1941), Courtesy of Tim Glick
Bottom: Page from 1920 catalog

Page from 1911 catalog (left)
and from 1912 catalog (below)

FARR'S
DELPHINIUMS
SELECTED
HYBRIDS

LONG-SPURRED COLUMBINES
GROWN AT WYOMISSING NURSERIES

Chapter 5

Phloxes, Delphiniums, Etc.

Hardy Plants have always appealed to me. They are the permanent features of the garden, and there is a personality and a sense of companionship about them that makes one grow attached to them.

—Bertrand H. Farr
Catalog, First Edition, 1908

In all of Farr's seven catalogs published between 1908 and 1920, before he began reducing the size of his catalogs and sending frequent newsletters, the page headings on the left read "Farr's Catalogue of Hardy Plant Specialties" (then "Catalogue" became "Book") and on the right, "Irises, Peonies, Phloxes, Delphiniums, Etc." – all in Olde English script. It is clear that the "Etc." plants took substantial space in the catalogs as well as in the nursery. Without attempting to cover all of the many plants under this abbreviated heading, this chapter will call attention to some of the plants on which Farr particularly comments.

Farr devotes a full page of descriptive and advisory text to Phloxes before listing, in his first catalog, the 168 varieties he is carrying. He emphasizes, "The *Phloxes* are, next to the peonies and iris, the most useful hardy plants we have, and for late summer and autumn blooming they are indispensable." And, "Their wide range of intensely brilliant colors include almost every shade but yellow in the most varied and striking combinations imaginable." All of these plants Farr imported, "embracing the choicest of Lemoine's latest introductions, and the best novelties by other European specialists."

About Delphiniums, Farr writes, "Its tall spires of bloom, rising to a height of five and six feet, supply our gardens with a blue that would be sadly lacking were it not for these magnificent plants." In addition to selling imported European varieties, which he mentions are not always perfect for hot, dry summers, he is also recommending his own "Wyomissing Hybrids," created to become more adaptable than the imports.

"In the dull November days, when every other flower in the garden has succumbed to the frost, the hardy Chrysanthemums hold sway, with a wealth of rich, oriental coloring unaffected by ordinary freezing." In a rare mixed metaphor for Farr, he compares colors of the flowers to an "old tapestry" and then places them in a "grand finale as the symphony of the garden ends under a mantle of snow."

Farr obviously takes pride in offering Tea Roses grown on their own roots in Wyomissing, but also in his large assortment of roses imported from "the most celebrated rose growers in the world," Dickson & Son, outside Belfast, Ireland. Founded in 1836 by Alexander Dickson, I, this firm has been famous for roses ever since, now managed by the sixth generation of Dicksons. Two of their now historic roses named on their website Farr listed in his catalog of 1908 – "Lady Helen Stewart" (1886) and "Hugh Dickson" (1904), both crimson with scarlet and highly perfumed. By his Sixth Edition Catalog of 1920, Farr has added substantially to his

Photo & caption from Farr's 1915 catalog

One of my plantings, a hedge of the magnificent white Rose, Frau Karl Druschki rose list and, in his proportionately longer essay writes about the "beautiful, fragrant blooms for home decoration" and other roses useful for landscaping, such as the "trailing Wichuraiana hybrids, with their slender branches, 20 to 30 feet in length," capable of "completely covering sloping banks, terraces or rocky places." He takes pride in his selection of roses, guided by observations in his own trial-grounds and by "advice from some of the best-informed rosarians," no doubt J. Horace McFarland, his publisher in Harrisburg and famous rosarian, being one of them. The rose section of the catalog begins, "A garden without Roses would be sadly deficient."

"Indispensable" is something Farr would likely have called all his Hardy Plant Specialties. They all have some desirable characteristics to be admired and taken advantage of somewhere in the garden and at sometime during the year. Like a good salesman, in one sense, but also a true gardener, he can explain the specific characteristics and qualities of each variety and its position in space and time in the garden calendar. He often contrasts growing conditions north and south of Philadelphia to recommend certain varieties. Or he describes various balances between size of bloom and length of bloom. Farr's knowledge and passion spring up throughout the catalogs.

In the first catalog of 1908, Farr writes, "I began the growing of Dahlias many years ago for my own pleasure, my enthusiasm leading me to try hundreds of varieties, every year adding all the prominent new ones that were offered. In offering this collection to the public, I have made a sweeping cut-out of every variety that is in the least doubtful as to its blooming qualities, or that shows any marked tendency to 'run out.'" Despite "a sweeping cut-out," the catalog still lists 110 varieties.

"Among the shrubs in every old garden, the Lilacs… have always been the chief feature, admired by all and universally loved for the many old associations and tender sentiment woven about them." Farr extols the work of Victor Lemoine, "probably the world's most skillful hybridizer," famous for his accomplishments with many different plants in Nancy, France, and, in particular, for his succession of new hybrid lilacs. Lemoine was assisted by his wife (who had better eyesight) and their son Emile and then his son Henri.

Farr cites Highland Park in Rochester, N.Y. as having the largest collection of lilacs in the United States and the Arnold Arboretum in Boston as having a similar collection. Highland Park was established as a gift from the prominent nurserymen George Ellwanger and Patrick Barry and then designed as an arboretum by Frederick Law Olmsted. In 1892 the first 20 lilacs were planted, and by 1897 the first Lilac Festival began, drawing, by Farr's time as he notes, 175,000 people in the spring. Arnold Arboretum, established by two gifts of land to Harvard University from Boston merchant Benjamin Bussey and from New Bedford whaling merchant James Arnold and also designed by Olmsted, began having its lilac festival called "Lilac Sunday" every second Sunday in May, now a hundred-year tradition.

Farr follows up in a paragraph of one sentence: "In my new specimen grounds, I have started a similar collection, and look forward with keen anticipation to a 'Lilac Time' in Wyomissing that will be well worth a visit." By 1920 he will have a collection of 90 different lilacs, and more will be coming.

Keeping Highland Park and the Arnold Arboretum in view again, as well as Lemoine, he credits Lemoine with accomplishing with Philadelphus, or mock orange, almost as much as he has with lilacs and remarks that in both parks "the collection of Philadelphus is second in importance only to that of the lilacs." In 1917 Farr lists 29 varieties of mock orange and 10 more to be supplied the next spring. He emphasizes the great variation in their foliage and overall size and their common refined beauty.

These shrubs were also part of

From Farr's 1922 catalog showing his landscape work with mock oranges at home of Henry Janssen on Reading Boulevard

From Farr's 1911 catalog with unidentified women in the Farrs' backyard and caption: *A quiet afternoon – the shrubbery border shielding the world within from the world without*

Farr's expansion of his landscaping business – selling more shrubs and trees and providing local and even national landscaping services. This interest was by no means a new one. In his 1917 catalog he writes, "Long before I sent out my first catalogue I designed and planted gardens for my friends. As I have a peculiar weakness for the smaller and more distinct evergreen trees, quite naturally I have used a great many of them in my own planting." This "weakness" for evergreens and other landscaping plants and increasing requests for his services led to expanding his catalog offerings of juniper, Japanese cypress, spruce, fir, magnolia, cherry, Japanese maple, and many other landscaping choices. He explains that in recent years, because he has "been called upon to help plan gardens in so many parts of the country," he is going public in his catalogs with his private lists. By 1924, Farr announces, "Our works have included the design and planting of home grounds, estates, parks, schools, factories, and other public and private institutions." By the early 1920's he had 150 acres of nursery stock and began hiring trained landscape managers to create the "Farr Landscape Department."

From Farr's 1920 catalog: *A well-planned Rock Garden, with its stone steps leading down to a pool fed by a cascade tumbling down the side of the rocks*

Also in this period, Farr began selling through his catalogs Niagara Dusting Materials, Niagara Soluble Sulphur Compound and the Niagara Hand-Blower Gun and the Hand-Dust Gun to combat problems like insects, fungus, San Jose scale, and oyster-shell scale. At the American Peony Society meeting in London, Ontario in 1922, he saw an exhibit for plant labels he admired and promptly "obtained the American agency for these labels." After working with the inventor to perfect his labels, Farr began offering these permanently-stamped aluminum labels in two sizes, made to custom orders.

Another exclusive arrangement concerns the hemerocallis, or daylily, another plant Farr had been steadily offering. He is credited with being one of the first in America to experiment with the hybridizing of daylilies. By 1924, to the 14 named varieties listed in his catalog, he added one new hybrid of his own (unnamed), promising "a strain with much larger, and more widely expanded flowers of most perfect form and great durability." In 1926, two years after Farr's death, the succeeding Farr Nursery catalog stated:

In recent years, Mr. Farr had turned his hand to the hybridization and improvement of the Hemerocallis. From his thousands of seedlings he selected and named about a dozen varieties with the same care and study which he applied to his iris introductions. During 1924, he discarded all but the best five, not because the other seven were poor, but because he wished to introduce only a very few Hemerocallis and wanted them to stand as "best" for many years. A few of them can be spared for 1926 shipment.

The five named were **Citronella, Lemon Queen, Mandarin, Golconda, and Ophir.** An unnamed daylily was also included as "the latest of all to bloom, continuing into September."

The exclusive arrangement with daylilies concerned one of the many friends Farr made in the horticultural world, Dr. Arlow B. Stout (1876-1957), Curator of Education and Laboratories at the New York Botanical Garden. Stout writes that Farr visited him frequently at the Garden, that Farr "was much interested in all our collections of hardy flowering plants" and that "he gave freely of such plants as the bearded and Japanese irises to increase the collections and make them more complete." Farr also "supplied a complete set of the various day lilies…in cultivation for use in the breeding work now under way in our experimental plots." These gifts coming from Farr and accepted by this prestigious botanical garden highlight the quality of Farr's plants as well as his collaborative spirit.

Hemerocallis citrina
Farr's New Hybrids

This is a very handsome new Chinese species, with beautiful light lemon-colored flowers, borne on very tall slender stems 4½ to 5 feet in height. The flowers in the species have the fault of not opening well, but by crossing these with one of the large-flowered kinds, I have produced a strain with much larger, and more widely expanded flowers of most perfect form and great durability. They are the latest of all to bloom, continuing until September. 40 cts. each, $3 for 10, $25 per 100.

Hemerocallis looks well along streams or moist banks

From Farr's 1924 catalog – though photo first used in his 1909 catalog and similar description used in 1917

Stout's experimental work during his 36 years at the Garden encompassed genetic studies on a wide range of plants like potatoes, peas and petunias and trees like apple, maple and date palm. However, he became most famous for his concentrated work with daylilies that multiplied the knowledge about daylilies, produced a host of new hybridized cultivars with many new colors and other attractions and, in turn, created an enormous surge in their popu-

Closeup of hemerocallis from 1909 photo

larity. In her book A *Passion for Daylilies*, Sydney Eddison asserts that "[i]ncontestably, Dr. Arlow Burdette Stout is the Father of the Modern Daylily."

She also characterizes Bertrand Farr as "a generous, indulgent courtesy uncle" of the daylily. Uncle Bert made a daylily deal with Stout that *was* generous on Farr's part and also so typical of him to want to have large collections of almost any hardy plant. Because the Garden's regulations prevented Stout from marketing the daylilies he was hybridizing, Farr agreed to grow the plants Stout would give him and later to sell the ones that met market standards. Eddison remarks that Farr's agreement "was altruistic" in relation to the conditions. Farr would have to do with daylilies what he had been doing with his own irises except for the hybridizing. As Eddison puts it, "Hundreds of the seedlings in his care would never qualify for introduction, but they would still require attention and occupy space at the nursery for several years during the trial period." Furthermore, one more condition was a lid on the price: "Stout cultivars would not be released until enough stock was on hand to keep the price down to $3 a division."

What actually happened, since Farr died shortly after this agreement was made, will be addressed in the last chapter. However, Farr's engagement with the daylily as a plant and with Dr. Stout as a partner is one more important example of Farr's wide-ranging interests and professional connections.

This chapter, of course, does not cover all of the large number of different plants in the Bertrand H. Farr – Wyomissing Nurseries Co. catalog. For the reader's interest, the index page of Farr's Seventh Edition Catalog of 1920-21, his last full-size catalog, is reproduced here.

Index

Index to Farr's 1920 catalog

74

Farr had another institutional connection as a member of the Pennsylvania Nurserymen's Association and as its President in 1917. Founded in 1904, this group was initially "concerned with the damaging affects of the San Jose Scale" and shortly later with lobbying for legislation on varied issues like requiring that pesticide products list their ingredients on the package, improving railroad delivery practices and keeping postal rates steady. When Farr was president, the annual meeting in Harrisburg that year was again concerned with plant diseases, but also with a public relations threat having to do with some public comments that, during this period of war, nurseries were non-essential. Rising to the defense of the nursery business, Bertrand Farr is quoted in a Harrisburg newspaper – a quotation that well defines him as the all-purpose and passionate nurseryman this chapter has tried to demonstrate he was:

> *No sane man will consider the nursery business as non-essential in the present struggle if he is careful to look at the subject before making such a statement. Fruit of all kinds is a food of the highest value, but the supply of such food depends primarily on the nurseryman who must grow and furnish the trees. Nor can America afford at this time to overlook the value and necessity of planting shade trees, evergreens, flowering shrubs, the beautiful roses whose colors match the stripes of the flag; the irises, peonies, phlox, whose blooms supply the fragrance and beauty needed to cheer and comfort those whose friends are engaged in the grim war. The gardener needs the rest and relaxation that comes from an intimate association with all these growing things.*

Aerial photo, Feb. 27, 1931. Upper area, City of Reading and Schuylkill River. Middle-right area, Borough of West Reading. Middle area, Wyomissing Industries buildings. Rest of area, Borough of Wyomissing. Bottom right, "The Circle" made by intersection of Wyomissing and Reading Boulevards.

Chapter 6

Wyomissing

In the first place, I think Wyomissing is very beautiful, surrounded on all sides by its setting of mountains. Through it flows the lovely stream which gives the town its name....
—Bertrand H. Farr
Catalog, Fifth Edition, 1915

"Wyomissing," a transliterated name from the Lenape Indian language meaning "Place of Flats" or "Place of Long Fish."

—Traditional

When Bertrand Farr bought some house lots in 1896, built a house and soon afterward moved from Reading with his new bride Anna to the suburb of Wyomissing, he could not have had any idea of the unusual town Wyomissing was to become, nor of the important people with whom he would connect there – textile men.

Just shortly after Farr had moved to Reading and established his piano-tuning business in 1891, two German immigrants also moved to Reading, rented a building and started a business in July 1892 to make braiding machines. The two men had emigrated independently from the same city in Germany a few years earlier and had been working for two different braid-making companies in Brooklyn and in New York. The late 19th century provided a big market for various types of narrow-fabric braid, especially for the bottom edges of women's long skirts, trim for hats and other apparel, as well as for shoelaces, elastic pieces for corsets, and laces for curtains.

From left to right: Ferdinand Thun, Henry Janssen and Gustav Oberlaender

Ferdinand Thun (1866-1949) and Henry Janssen (1866-1948) were born in a city that was a center of the braiding industry in Germany and

77

were born within six days of each other in February 1866, less than 16 months after Farr was born. In Barmen, Germany (now part of the consolidated City of Wuppertal) Thun had a business education; and Janssen, a technical one. As immigrants in New York, where they met each other for the first time, they recognized each other's complementary strengths and decided to become partners and take advantage of recent legislation putting a tariff on German-made braiding machines (the only ones in use in America at the time) and to begin making American ones. They decided to do so in Reading because Thun earlier had worked as an apprentice for a short time in a woolen mill near Reading (where he had met his future wife) and had become familiar with the dynamic industry there and its populous German-American work force. Furthermore, both Barmen and Reading had similar populations of around 80,000 and similar geography with a river and hilly terrain.

By that key year of 1896, their braiding-machine business emerged from its start-up difficulties and began expanding as orders came in. Thun and Janssen started looking for a way to move out of their small rented building in Reading. The Reading Suburban Real Estate Company, laying out streets on the farmland that was to become Wyomissing, struck a deal with these promising business partners – for one dollar Thun and Janssen were given some land on which to build their expanding Textile Machine Works. This one-dollar deal was the ignition for creating a major American enterprise and turning Wyomissing into a most unusual company town.

Within the ten-year period of 1896 to 1906, Thun and Janssen created the base from which their Wyomissing Industries would become the dominant industry in their textile field in the United States. Continuing in Wyomissing with making braiding machines, as they had in been doing in Reading, the two partners soon started up a narrow fabric company to make narrow fabrics with their own machines. Then they began making knitting machines for full-fashioned women's hosiery (the style in that 1900's era, with seams down the back and with fitted feet), and by 1906, knitting the stockings from their machines. The Wyomissing Industries now was composed of the Textile Machine Works, the Berkshire Knitting Mills and the Narrow Fabric Company.

In the meantime Thun and Janssen had built homes and moved to Wyomissing. In 1902 they established the Wyomissing Suburban Building and Loan Association, a bank for savings, mortgages, and real estate development. This bank, through a long succession of acquisitions and mergers, has now become Sovereign Bank with its headquarters still in Wyomissing. Thun

Street scenes in Wyomissing in 1942. Upper photo: Wyomissing Boulevard at Reading Boulevard looking northeast. Lower photo: Wyomissing Boulevard at Garfield Avenue looking south.

and Janssen, of course, were among the prominent men in Wyomissing, who, along with Bertrand Farr, were preparing the way for the incorporation of Wyomissing as a borough in 1906. Elected to the new Borough Council, and re-elected repeatedly, Thun served as its president from 1906 to 1944; and Janssen, as a member, from 1906 until his death in 1948. Farr served for a short time as the first burgess and later as a replacement councilman to fill an unexpired term. In 1912 he is listed as one of the nine Directors of Thun and Janssen's bank.

While Farr was busy leasing vacant lots in Wyomissing, growing plants, importing plants, hybridizing plants, and issuing extensive catalogs, the Wyomissing Industries men were rapidly expanding their textile business. Contained by thoughtful zoning, the Industries area nevertheless had plenty of room for its steady expansion of manufacturing and support operations on the north side of Wyomissing, separated neatly by a kind of buffer zone and the main east-west Penn Avenue from the residential, recreational, and horticultural areas of the developing town. The Berkshire Knitting Mills was on its way to becoming the largest full-fashioned hosiery producer in the world. By 1922 it was employing over 2,000 workers and making more than 12 million pairs of silk stockings a year. (By 1936, there were 6,000 workers at Berkshire.) In this 1920's period, the Textile Machine Works was on its way to supplying almost two-thirds of all the knitting machines used for stockings in the United States. The famous "Reading" Full-Fashioned Knitting Machine had 130,000 parts, all of which the Wyomissing Industries made in their own foundry and machine shops. (Their huge foundry, with spare capacity, also made parts for a wide range of other large industries – from power plants to automobiles to phonographs.)

Before the more modern style of campus-like industrial plants, these German-Americans "wanted their industrial 'park' to complement the residential 'park' of Wyomissing." Sensitive to having a clean, neat, and aesthetically pleasing environment both inside and outside their buildings, they used a tunnel system to hide all the utility lines and facilitate transport between buildings. They landscaped buildings and open areas with cherry trees and various shrubs, which probably came from Farr's nursery. (In 1914 Farr drew up detailed landscape plans for Janssen's new Wyomissing home on Reading Boulevard, plans which included 104 kinds of trees and shrubs.) The many different company buildings – manufacturing, office, garage, cafeteria, dispensary and library – were attractively laid out and designed and, inside, were clean and well-lit.

On the south side of Penn Avenue, where Farr lived and had his nursery, Thun and

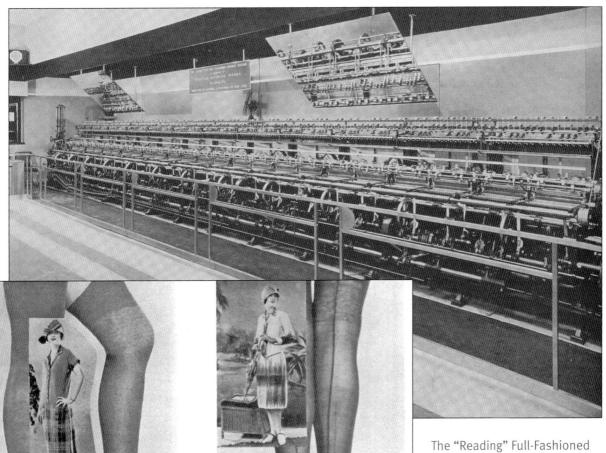

1918

The silk boot was increased to three-quarter length. Principally 39 gauge and with plaited heel, sole and toe construction.

1922

Pointex heels appeared. The gauge was gradually increased to 42. Three-quarter silk boot still in vogue. Use of rayon started in 1924.

The "Reading" Full-Fashioned Knitting Machine made by the Textile Machine Works and used by the Berkshire Knitting Mills and many other knitting companies around the world. Photo, 1936

From "Looking Back Over Berkshire's Hosiery's Styles" in the company's inhouse March 1934 magazine *The Yarn Carrier*

Janssen, as borough councilmen and businessmen, were building on what the original developers had begun in 1896. At that time, as the streets were being laid out in Wyomissing, less than one square mile in area then, the Reading Suburban Development Company had 2,400 trees planted along the streets, thereby beginning a long tradition of beautiful trees and well-managed tree care, a tradition these two men helped to maintain. As their wealth grew, they generously contributed their money and used their political positions to help build schools, playgrounds, a swimming pool, and a library in Wyomissing as well as a general hospital and a combined natural history, ethnographic and art museum next door. Initially for their executives and later opened for public membership, Thun and Janssen built an eating club and, in honor of Farr, named it "The Iris Club." In the meantime, these extremely enterprising men were busy starting another bank, the People's Trust Company, and creating mixed-income housing for their employees and others through their Delta Realty Corporation and their Wyomissing Development Company.

Rear view of The Iris Club (front on Fairview Avenue)

In 1906, as the Berkshire Knitting Mills was just beginning, Thun and Janssen, to help run their stocking business, hired another German-American immigrant they had known well during their days in New York. Gustav Oberlaender (1867-1936) managed the business well, becoming an expert especially in the selection and purchase of silk and in techniques of dyeing silk. In 1912 Oberlaender built a substantial house next to the Farrs, just on the other corner of Wyomissing Boulevard and Dauphin Avenue. He must have been an interesting neighbor for Farr, though there is no evidence of horticultural interchange between them. A few years after Farr died in 1924, Oberlaender retired from Berkshire with about seven million dollars and began using his money to travel, to collect fine art, and to contribute to the German Archaeological Institute in Berlin for its projects in Athens and in Pergamon, Turkey and to the University of Pennsylvania for archaeology in Minturnae, Italy. Some objects from these three projects are now exhibited in the Reading Public Museum.

Building on an international exchange idea that Ferdinand Thun had initiated, Oberlaender then established in 1931 the Oberlaender Trust with one million dollars, all of it, under the unusual condition for a charitable trust, to be spent within 25 years. Its purpose was to promote German-American friendships and professional knowledge exchanges between German and American adults such as foresters, municipal-department heads, public health workers, teachers, and journalists. Bertrand Farr, had he still been alive, would have been a prime candidate to be an Oberlaender Fellow. Initially, the exchange worked mostly by making grants to Americans going to Germany, though there was one particular German who won two Oberlaender Fellowships to come to America – Albert Einstein. After Hitler and conditions in Germany disrupted the original plan, the Trust money was used to bring more than 300 German professors to America and to help them secure teaching positions in colleges and universities all over the country.

These three enterprising, civic and philanthropic men – Thun, Janssen, and Oberlaender – were a critical part of the context of Bertrand Farr's life in Wyomissing. Wyomissing, as a town, it should be remembered, was small, especially compared to the growing Wyomissing Industries textile "town" across Penn Avenue. When Wyomissing was incorporated in 1906, just two years before Farr issued his first catalog, the town was less than a square mile (510 acres) with a population under 400. In Farr's death year of 1924, the town had grown through annexation to about one-and-a-half square miles (992 acres) and had a population less than 3,000. Thun and Janssen, as borough councilman, were helping the town to grow through annexation of abutting, mostly open land. As private citizens, separately they bought hundreds of acres of nearby open farm land for their interests in growing apples and raising cattle and in having a "country place." As the officers of their Wyomissing Development Company, they would acquire most of the land in Farr's nursery.

Exactly how they managed to do so is the Secret of the next chapter.

Scenes along the Wyomissing Creek, from 1915 catalog

The meadow is framed by the woodland

An ideal place for a water-garden

A brook hurries through the grass

Through it flows the lovely Wyomissing stream

84

Here I am planning a new garden to contain all the choicest shrubs and plants grown at Wyomissing, where they may develop into mature specimens—my Dream Garden, the beauties of which, if it comes true, I hope to share with all my friends and visitors

Chapter 7

The Later Years

We dance round in a ring and suppose,
But the Secret sits in the middle and knows.

—Robert Frost

Having operated a nursery mostly on leased land in a variety of locations, in 1913 Bertrand Farr purchased a significant amount of land he now could call his own. By the end of 1913 he had 73 acres of fields in an area that the Borough of Wyomissing would later annex and that would be developed into a residential area known as "Birdland." He also owned a few house lots and a very special five-acre section of former Philip Evans meadow land along the Wyomissing Creek in an area east of the nearby Old Mill, which Evans had built in 1767.

In January 1915, in the Introduction to the Fifth Edition of his Catalog, he announces his having acquired nursery land "beautifully situated within ten minutes' walk from my present buildings and grounds." He exults particularly about the smaller parcel he now owns along the Wyomissing Creek and the wonderful dreams he has for this area:

> *Through [Wyomissing] flows the lovely stream which gives the town its name,*
> *and here, on both sides, I hope to plant a specimen garden, where some of each*
> *of the hundreds of varieties of Peonies, Irises, Phloxes, etc., and all of the shrubs*
> *and trees grown in Wyomissing may be concentrated and artistically arranged.*

Lovingly, he describes the broad setting of Wyomissing as "very beautiful, surrounded on all sides by its setting of mountains," and then the specific, enchanting setting for this special garden he calls his Dream Garden:

> *The meadow is framed in by the woodland and divided by the Wyomissing Creek.*
> *A little brook hurries through the tall grass. There are springs clear as crystal, and*
> *a little pond, all furnishing ideal conditions for a water-garden. There will be a*
> *Lilac and Iris, a Peony and a Rose time, and so on throughout the season, if it all*
> *comes true, as I hope. And, when it does, I hope you can all come to see it.*

Farr's next catalog, the Sixth Edition of 1917 for the Season of 1918, reports that his Dream Garden "will be many years before it is fully developed, but the dream is gradually coming true."

> *The Lilac collection of 100 or more varieties is becoming well established....*
> *The Peony walk has been a joy to hundreds of visitors. Just now the collection of*
> *Philadelphus, or Mock Oranges, is at its best. There are very complete collections*
> *of Loniceras, Deutzias, Viburnums, and other shrubs, Flowering Crabs,*
> *Magnolias, and Japanese Cherries.*

Farr says nothing more about a water-garden, but Catharine Keiser Reed, the woman mentioned in Chapter 1, whose father was Farr's stableman, does remember the spring that sent a narrow stream into what, as a little girl, she used to call the "Great Lakes" but now describes as one lake composed of three arms, along with an island or two and Japanese-style bridges. What very likely is the same spring emerges today inside a residential yard at Thrush Road and Parkside Drive South and down into an oval pond in the same yard and then out underground into the nearby Wyomissing Creek.

Catharine remembers walking through the peonies in the Dream Garden and recalls that Farr's barn, which held his six horses, was painted yellow. She also remembers frequent visitors to the nursery, especially two of them. One day Mary Pickford and Charlie Chaplin appeared to buy plants, and Catharine supplied the water for Charlie's dog to drink.

John Wister writes about visiting Farr and his nursery several times and describes the Dream Garden as being on a "sloping piece of ground covering several acres, beginning at the lowest point in the nursery [the part above the Dream Garden] and running downward to the stream [the Wyomissing Creek]. Curved walks, twenty or more feet wide, ran along the edges and to either side were specimen lilacs, deutzias, philadelphus, and peonies. ... Above this Dream Garden there were, for many years, great blocks of irises, sometimes acres in extent and it was a wonderful sight to see the masses of color in the blooming season."

*I*n 1915 Farr writes, "[W]hat began as a hobby has become a business that grows so rapidly that it requires the utmost effort to keep pace with it." Judging from his earlier catalogs and horticultural efforts, one might fairly conclude that the hobby had become a business well before 1915, operating under various names – "Farr's Hardy Plants," then "Wyomissing Nursery" and later "Wyomissing Nurseries." However, in 1916 Farr's nursery officially became a business when he incorporated it under the name "Bertrand H. Farr – Wyomissing Nurseries Co." Apparently this move to incorporation was not his idea. He explains in his 1917 catalog:

> *One day a friend said: 'Why don't you incorporate and let us help you? Not that we want to make money, but we feel that Wyomissing, and you, and the fields of flowers are inseparable, and we, who have the interests of the place so much at heart, want to see you succeed to greater things. We want to see you free to carry on the work among the plants, for which you are best fitted, relieved of the drudgery of mere detail and routine by a competent organization.'*

The identity of this particular "friend" is likely to remain a Secret, but one can suppose that the use of the plural "we" and "interests of the place" strongly suggests a group, and that group must have been the Wyomissing Development Company, the company formed by the Wyomissing Industries textile men in 1913 to buy real estate and to construct and sell houses in the eastern end of Wyomissing and farther east in abutting West Reading and a section of Reading known as the 18th Ward. Four of the incorporating stockholders in Farr's nursery company were officials from the development company – Ferdinand Thun, President, and Henry Janssen, Vice-president, each with a hundred shares, and Gustav Oberlaender, Treasurer, and Philip Zieber, the firm's lawyer, each with ten shares.

As will become apparent, it is likely that Farr's report of his friend's offer above omits most of what probably was a much more complicated arrangement between Farr and the developers.

Incorporated for $150,000 with 1500 shares of par value of $100, with Farr holding half of the shares, his business was presumably now poised to enable him to realize bigger and better plans for his nursery: "Now with ample fields and sufficient help, I seem to stand again on a pyramid, from whose height, as in those early days [in Iowa], the horizon appears filled with a promise of new and larger opportunities…that with the means at hand, I may be able to grow, not only enough plants for all, but larger and finer ones than ever before."

Farr's reference to "ample fields" comes from his having made two large purchases. Immediately after the incorporation on March 30, 1916, Farr passed papers on March 31 with Isaac Hoffa for 89 acres of land and again on May 1 with the heirs of Thomas Schwartz for another 93 acres.

Farr's office and greenhouse, 1250 Garfield Avenue. Undated photo from Farr Nursery collection.

These two contiguous fields were spread in an irregular, elongated way over areas near and across what is now Museum Road. This land was in the 18th Ward of Reading and what then was abutting Cumru Township (before annexed by Wyomissing) and extended across the Wyomissing Creek into a small piece of West Reading. Then on May 11 Farr sold his various holdings to his company, a total of about 265 acres, counting his fields and his house lots. Despite, however, the investment funds that came in from the incorporation, both these purchases were heavily mortgaged.

Farr, above, also mentions "sufficient help." Although the accompanying photographs are undated and are probably from the early 1920's, they show the sizeable office staff (23) and field force (45 or so) Farr had been building. Farr's catalog of 1912 includes a picture of his 25 x 150 feet greenhouse built that year, and another undated picture shows the office building next to this greenhouse at 1250 Garfield Avenue (still there as a private residence). In his main catalogs and order forms from 1908 to 1924, he never used a street address, just the town name. In Wyomissing Nurseries advertisements placed in a variety of other publications, six other addresses appear, all on Garfield Avenue – 103,104,106,126,and 500 – all probably code numbers for the ads and not representing actual buildings.

Photo of Farr's greenhouse, 1250 Garfield Avenue, from 1912 catalog

Farr needed considerable resources for both his developing local landscape business and his largely mail order business. For mail orders, Farr's catalogs were both critical and expensive. Well-designed, sturdy, and extensive, they were published in Harrisburg, Pennsylvania by the man whose company "had become America's premier publisher of gardening catalogs." J. Horace McFarland (1859-1948) experimented with color printing, and some of his company's catalogs may have had "the first color photographs produced in the US." Farr took advantage of this new opportunity as examples in this book show. McFarland's firm also produced a set of about 100 tinted glass slides of Farr's flowers and plants for Farr to show with the talks he used to give to various horticultural groups.

McFarland, himself, was famous for his active commitments to conservation, campaigning to establish the National Park Service and then to protect some of the new national parks that faced major threats. In 1904, he became the first president of the American Civic Association, fighting urban blight and promoting natural beauty in America's cities. A nationally

Photo of Farr's office staff taken 1923 or 1924. Second row: Lester W. Needham, left end, and Harold G. Seyler, right end. Third row: Charles M. Boardman, right end – the three men who bought the nursery in 1925

Photo of Farr's field forces taken along Reading Boulevard with residence of Henry Janssen in background

prominent horticulturist, especially for the roses he grew in Harrisburg, McFarland was a founder and the president of the American Rose Society, and also had a "famous testing ground for hundreds of new plant species…[containing] 5,000 plants including varieties of roses." McFarland and Farr must have been each other's customers and good friends as well. At Farr's death, McFarland wrote,

> *Anyone who had to do with Mr. Farr many times in many years, as I had,*
> *would agree with me not only as to the pleasure of the personal contact, but as*

Undated photo of Farr's trucks taken along Reading Boulevard, from Farr Nursery collection

to his possession of that something beyond rules, formulas and experience which reached into the heart of plant life in a fashion that made intercourse a keen pleasure to anyone fortunate enough to have it. He was a truly great plantsman, and he has left among the garden folks of America a great record of acute plant inspiration joined with rugged honesty.

After all of these positive experiences of Farr's nursery life – the incorporation, the real estate purchases, the expanding of his many hardy plant collections, the frequent visitors to his nursery, the beginnings of his Dream Garden, the friend's encouragement (as Farr cites) for him and his flowers to be an "inseparable" part of Wyomissing – it should come as a surprise that only five years later Farr was selling his nursery land and two more years later was starting to move his whole business 12 miles west from Wyomissing to the country town of Womelsdorf because the development company men had purchased his nursery for residential development.

Some key questions now arise. Was Farr forced out? or eased out? or what? When and how did he learn about the necessity, or the chance, to move? How did he feel about a move? What kind of conversations did he have with his stockholders, especially the men from the development company? The Secret sitting in the middle is not going to provide any definitive answers, but the following sketchy narrative will dance around and eventually offer some suppositions.

In 1917, just one year after Farr had incorporated his nursery and made his two large land purchases, the Wyomissing Development Company (WDC) engaged the prominent town planning firm of Hegemann & Peets, based in Milwaukee, to create a plan for the eastern end of Wyomissing and parts of West Reading and the 18th Ward in Reading – a real estate development within these three contiguous political areas to be marketed as "Wyomissing Park." Much of Farr's nursery was within this area. Presumably, then, Farr must have known that at some point fairly soon he was going to lose the land he had just bought.

Werner Hegemann (1881-1936) and Elbert Peets (1886-1968) only gradually developed the plan; but contact was maintained between Hegemann and, for the Wyomissing men, Irvin F. Impink (1882-1963). Impink, the Secretary of the WDC, was also its contractor-builder, who, in his

career from 1916 to 1935, would build over 500 houses for the company, some of the more expensive ones on Farr's former land. Impink would also build the Reading Hospital in West Reading and the Reading Public Museum , both on land donated by Ferdinand Thun and Impink and with generous funds donated by Thun, Henry Janssen and Gustav Oberlaender. A complication here is that Impink and Thun had a real estate partnership that was, in effect, an agency for their own WDC.

In 1918 a letter from Impink advises Hegemann, a German national, not to come at that time to Wyomissing because of the intense anti-German feelings and riots in the Reading area resulting from World War I. Impink then writes:

> *As to the Farr Nursery property, we understand that you have not as yet done any work in this plan and since the Nursery is at this time very severely handicapped by present conditions, we would advise that you do nothing on their plans until we have had a chance to discuss this entire matter with you.*

Top: Werner Hegemann
Bottom: Irvin F. Impink

The "severely handicapped" part of the letter probably refers to financial difficulties Farr would have been having with heavy debt, with lower consumer demand during this last part of the war, and with issues stemming from the recent Import Exclusion Act, which cut off his supply of plants from abroad. As for the "plans," they were not delayed very long. In 1919 Hegemann and Peets issued ground plans, descriptions, and town-planning philosophy in a booklet written by Hegemann titled "Wyomissing Park: The Modern Garden Suburb of Reading, Pennsylvania, A Stepping Stone Towards a Greater Reading." Although the street plan was much less detailed for the area Farr owned than for elsewhere, at the eastern end of his fields the plan called for a Farr Boulevard, which would have been extended as a main thoroughfare through West Reading and connected to Penn Avenue.

Hegemann had proposed more ideas than WDC wanted to implement, including a golf course running along both sides of the Wyomissing Creek and a business and theatre center in West Reading. Nevertheless, WDC did begin carrying out some of the planners' ideas for preserving park lands; creating small, green enclaves within residential areas; avoiding street layouts on a grid and building houses in the western section of so-called Wyomissing Park. In this 1919 to 1921 period, Farr's land, in the eastern section, remained unplanned.

On May 3, 1921, however, the WDC minutes read, "After discussing the advisability of purchasing the Farr Nursery Farms, it was decided to await further developments." Then, from the minutes of October 8, "Mr. Janssen brought before the meeting the matter of the purchase by Messrs. Thun and Impink of about ninety (90) acres of the Farr Nurseries property." The minutes conclude that "it was decided to leave the matter open for future adjustment." This "future adjustment" was made almost immediately – just three days later on October 11 Farr sold his 89-acre former Isaac Hoffa land to Thun and Impink. On the same day in 1921, Thun sold back to Farr the 36 acres of Schwartz land he had, for some unknown reason bought from Farr in 1919.

The next year on August 2, 1922, Ferdinand Thun bought back that 36 acres plus all the rest of Farr's main nursery land, a total of 164 acres. Combined with the 89-acre field bought in 1921, the WDC men now owned 253 acres of the Farr nursery. All that was left were 10 house lots on Reading Boulevard behind the nursery office and greenhouse on Garfield Avenue, and Farr sold off these lots to a private buyer at about the same time in 1922; a few other house lots plus the office and greenhouse were sold after Farr's death.

Two conditions in these transactions are important. One is that most, if not actually all, of Farr's nursery stock was excluded in the sales of his land, thereby giving Farr some time to deal with his many plants. The other condition lies in the deed records that show Farr was carrying a combined mortgage load of over $38,000 in 1916 at the time of the transfer of his land to his corporation. By 1922, at the time of the final sale to Ferdinand Thun, the total had been reduced to over $17,000, still a good sum for Farr to have deducted from the unrecorded selling price.

The WDC minutes of April 20, 1922, three months before the final purchase of the Farr land, state, "Mr. Impink asked the opinion of the Board of Directors as to the opening of the Farr Boulevard and building of homes on it, to conform with the third avenue houses." The contractor's eagerness to get going on the Farr land was restrained by the other directors. Not fully satisfied with the plans Hegemann and Peets had made, the directors were in the process of hiring an even more famous town planner to draw up new plans, especially for the Farr nursery part of the property, for which Hegemann and Peets had incomplete plans.

John Nolen

John Nolen (1869-1937) is regarded as America's first town planner and its preeminent one during the early 1900's. By the end of his career, he and his firm in Cambridge, Massachusetts had over 350 city and town planning commissions across the United States from San Diego, California to Milwaukee, Wisconsin to Charlotte, North Carolina as well as one in Reading, Pennsylvania in 1910. By the time Nolen and the Wyomissing Development Company issued the 20-page booklet of descriptions and plans for Wyomissing Park, Hegemann's "Farr Boulevard" had been reduced to a shorter and narrower "Farr Road."

The hiring and the subsequent work of these town planners raises additional questions about Farr's relationship with and attitude toward them. Here the Secret releases clues inside part of a letter Farr wrote in 1924 to the newspaper in Webster City:

> We [here in Wyomissing] have a very progressive lot of people who are laying out the suburban surroundings under the direction of Mr. John Nolan [sic], of Cambridge, Mass., probably the most celebrated city planning expert in the United States. I have called their attention to the beautiful effect of your wide streets with unusually wide parking plots on either side and comparatively narrow driveway.

The whole tone here is certainly positive about what is the real estate development of his former nursery land. Farr is referring to the Wyomissing Development Company as "a very progressive lot of people," and he apparently was giving to these developers and even to John Nolen advice based on Webster City street design.

Then, later in 1924, just before his death, in a nursery newsletter he finally reveals for the first time that he is moving the nursery, but also expresses very positive attitudes about the move to Womelsdorf in relation to the disadvantages of the disconnected, scattered nursery layout in the Wyomissing area versus the advantages of the new, more centralized location on a highly visible main highway.

Given this evidence coming from these various sources between 1916 and 1924, one could suppose the following. The development men in Wyomissing in 1916, or earlier, arranged with Farr to help him incorporate his business and thereby help him to buy land, much of which he had already been renting for several years, thereby securing the land for Farr – and for the developers — until such time as they wanted to build on it. Helping Farr also may have made it easier for them to buy the land from Farr rather than from the previous owners. The last step in this scenario might have been the developers' help in locating new and improved nursery space for Farr, as it turned out, in Womelsdorf.

In the meantime, developments within the American Peony Society and the newly organized American Iris Society were also affecting Farr and his nursery, all having to do with rating each variety. Over a period of several years, starting in 1916, members of the Peony Society began a series of "symposiums" that facilitated the members' rating of peonies on a scale of 10, the publishing of the tabulated results, and then creating a double effect on nurserymen. First, in their advertising they began identifying and promoting those varieties that had scored high. But, second, they began discarding or selling at bargain prices the varieties that had scored low.

Influenced by the increasing cultivation of irises in America, by the growing numbers of iris articles and publications, and by the successes of the Peony Society, some irisarians (including people from the Peony Society) decided to establish the American Iris Society. On January 29, 1920 the founding meeting was held at the New York Botanical Garden. Among the important attendees were John Wister (famous for his work with tree peonies), Lee Bonnewitz (then the current president of the Peony Society) and Bertrand Farr (still a director of the Peony Society). At this first organizational meeting, Wister was elected as the Society's first president; and Farr was elected a director and given positions on three committees: nominating, publicity, and test and exhibition gardens.

Among the Iris Society's first objectives was to follow the lead of the Peony Society by completing the work Wister and a few others had begun to eliminate the nomenclature confusion in irises and then to establish quality ratings for individual varieties. Through a series of published checklists and through test gardens, the Iris Society moved quickly to accomplish the first phases of these objectives.

Quickly enough, so that by October 1, 1922 in the Introduction to Farr's newly formatted catalog called *Better Plants – By Farr*, he writes that his nursery has dropped from his catalog and "will discard upwards of two hundred varieties" of peonies and irises. He cites the "remarkable work" of the two Societies and explains that he has used their rating systems to drop varieties judged less than six out of a possible ten points. In his second new catalog, dated February 1, 1924, Farr writes, "I have set a still higher standard in the Peony and Iris lists by eliminating all varieties rating less than seven out of a possible ten points. This means the discarding of ninety-three additional varieties besides the two hundred or more varieties dropped in the first edition."

Nevertheless. he saw as an opportunity what most people probably would regard as a loss. This optimist and master collector of plants writes that this discarding of lower ranking plants "allows space for the addition of …new introductions, which had to be omitted in last year's book."

Included in the iris section of this 1924 catalogue, Bertrand Farr's last one, is a quotation from an article in the magazine *The Flower Grower* written by R.S. Sturtevant, Secretary of the Iris Society, and a telling commentary on Farr's leadership as a nurseryman:

> *Mr. Farr was the first Iris specialist in this country; his classification into sections set a high standard for many years, and his introductions find a proper place in even the smallest gardens. He was the first to list Irises in hundreds of varieties, and he is now the first to discard poor varieties in a wholesale way. Others may refrain from listing poorly rated things, but he has actually junked them and set an example which we hope other growers will follow.*

OFFICERS AND JUDGES, NEW ROCHELLE, 1923
Standing, left to right: Mrs. L.W. Hitchcock, Mrs. Theodore I. Coe, Miss F.E. McIlvaine, Mrs. W.H. Peckham,
Arthur Harrington, Mrs. J.J. Montague, Miss Mary C. Bissell, Mrs. George V. Nash.
Seated: Mrs. Charles Pratt, Mrs. W.R. Pierson, Frank H. Presby, John C. Wister, R.S. Sturtevant,
Mrs. C.S. McKinney, Bertrand H. Farr, Harry A. Norton
Photo & caption from American Iris Society Bulletin, Jan. 1925

These later years in Bertrand Farr's life, from around 1916 to 1923, like his earlier years, encompassed challenges for Farr that excite curiosity about how he met them.. Earlier, the questions would be about the challenges of teaching school, of trying to be a serious pianist, of running a music store in Webster City or Reading. In 1916 the change to an incorporated business raises questions about how he related to his stockholders and adjusted to running a more structured business. Economic and other conditions surrounding World War I and then the new standards from the Iris and the Peony Societies causing him to discard many plants – these forces all must have had financial and psychological effects. And, near the end, the move to Womelsdorf very likely produced conflicting feelings. Despite the advantages Farr cites for the move there, what regrets did he have about giving up what he had so lovingly pioneered in Wyomissing? There is rich material here for a biographical novel.

From 1924 catalog: *Farr's Peonies displayed at the Colonial Trust Company, Reading, Penna., June, 1923*

Chapter 8

The Last Year

It was his task to glorify nature and he performed it well.

—*Webster City Daily News*, Oct. 13, 1924

Before Farr died in October, the year 1924 was eventful for him and for his community. He would be traveling a lot, continuing the move of his nursery to Womelsdorf, and donating his Dream Garden and other plants. For the story of that donation, it is necessary to turn to events in the City of Reading and the development of the Reading Public Museum.

The founder and first director of the museum, Levi Mengel (1868-1941), one could say with some seriousness, initiated it when he was just a little boy growing up in Reading in the 1870's and collecting things like bugs and butterflies, rocks and minerals. By the time he graduated from high school in 1886, Mengel was reported to have 5,000 natural history items in his personal collection. After a mix of experiences studying pharmacy, accompanying Lt. Robert Peary on an expedition to Greenland, running the Old Mill in Wyomissing as a flour mill, and helping to form the Reading Suburban Real Estate Company, he became a science teacher in Reading Boys' High School. Dedicated to visual learning and hands-on teaching, he began using objects from his own vast collections and, then, in 1904, multiplied his collection by negotiating the purchases and the gifts of almost 2,000 items from the international exhibitors at the end of the St. Louis World's Fair, museum quality cultural objects mostly from Asian and Central and South American countries.

Photo of Reading Public Museum from 1930, shortly after opening in 1928

Plaque inside the museum honoring Levi Mengel

1868   1941

IN MEMORY OF

LEVI W. MENGEL Sc.D. L.L.D.

SCIENTIST • EDUCATOR • PHILANTHROPIST

FOUNDER OF THE READING PUBLIC MUSEUM AND ART GALLERY

"THE BEST WAY TO FIND THE MEANING OF THINGS
IS TO BEGIN TO KNOW BY PERSONAL EXPERIENCE."

By 1907 the combination of Mengel's expanding personal collection and this World's Fair collection – scientific and cultural objects plus, later on, fine art – became a "museum" on the third floor of the Reading School District building to be used extensively for the education of Reading's students. By 1924 Mengel's collection had taken over all three floors of the District building, and the City was eager to build a proper museum building. However, the issue of where to place it created a virtual storm of controversy. To the rescue, in a sense, came Ferdinand Thun and Irvin Impink, representing their real estate partnership and their Wyomissing Development Company.

On July 3, 1924, in big headlines in the *Reading Eagle* came the announcement:

PARK AND MUSEUM SITE OFFERED TO CITY AS GIFT

55 ACRES ALONG WYOMISSING CREEK IN 18TH WARD EMBRACED IN TENDER

DONORS STAND READY TO IMPROVE TRACT AT OWN EXPENSE AND ESTABLISH BOTANICAL GARDEN AND ARBORETUM – ENGAGE EXPERT TO PREPARE PLANS

The lengthy article that followed explained the many advantages of the offer of this land along the Wyomissing Creek, the already existing native trees, the promise of the donors to take care of all the site development and landscaping, and the strong approval by city planner John Nolen for this "opportunity of unusual merit" for the citizens of Reading. Because this site, close by Farr's former nursery land, existed in the so-called 18th Ward, a small section of Reading on the west side of the Schuylkill River, the new museum would be divided from the main part of city and the schools on the east side. To meet this transportation problem, the article explained that an anonymous donor was going to provide regular bus service for students.

Special emphasis in the article was on the offer by Bertrand Farr of his Dream Garden to help establish a botanical garden and arboretum: "Mr. Impink announced that Bertrand H. Farr, president of the Wyomissing Nurseries Company, Inc., has offered the extensive and varied assortment of trees, shrubs and flowering plants from his "Dream Garden", along the Wyomissing road, as a nucleus for the botanical garden and arboretum...." Later, the article began to identify Farr's gift collection:

> *Included in the Farr collection are lilacs, peonies and iris, which enjoy a*
> *nation-wide reputation. Among the other trees, shrubs and flowering plants*
> *in the "Dream Garden" are phlox, delphinium, mock orange, willow oak,*
> *rhododendron, Japanese maple, purple beech, several varieties of willow,*
> *dogwood, several varieties of birch, hawthorn, fir, hemlock, spruce, pine,*
> *juniper, magnolia, and many varieties of climbing roses. There are nearly*
> *300 varieties of peonies alone in the "Dream Garden."*

After further controversy in Reading in the wake of the bold announcement in this article, the School Board voted to accept the whole offer of land and plants. (The area of land was later reduced to 25 acres.) By September, just one month before Farr's death, the landscape architect for the coming project, Elmer A. Muhs, wrote to Nolen's firm in Cambridge that he had gone through the Dream Garden with Mr. Farr, making a list of plants and noting his and Farr's judgments of their desirability. Muhs concludes, "In addition to the Dream Garden material, Mr. Farr handed us a list of shrubs in his nursery fields which are also available as a part of the collection. We feel that both lists amount to quite a bulk of planting material and that they will undoubtedly go a long way toward building up a very creditable Botanical Garden."

*E*arlier that year, on April 1 was recorded the purchase by the Wyomissing Nurseries Company for $20,000 of land in Womelsdorf, which was to become the new home of Farr's nursery about 12 miles west of Wyomissing. This 140-acre property came with the condition that 24 of the acres plus several historic buildings be excepted and conveyed to the Conrad Weiser Memorial Park Association. This property, then about to become a state park, was dedicated in honor of Conrad Weiser, famous pioneer settler, Indian interpreter and agent, and judge. The address for the nursery at its beginning there was William Penn Highway, Weiser Park, Womelsdorf, the highway being the main route from Philadelphia through Reading and Wyomissing and Womelsdorf to Harrisburg.

The nursery and Conrad Weiser Park properties, were, and still are, just outside the eastern edge of Womelsdorf, a town of about 1,200 in 1924. In that year the cigar industry in Womelsdorf was still flourishing with a factory making cigar boxes and with over ten other "factories" employing from five to a hundred people making cigars, mostly home-based folks rolling the cigars. The man who sold the land to Farr was Leroy Valentine, the main owner of the cigar business in Womelsdorf.

In February, 1923, Farr began sending out periodic four-page newsletters titled "Better Plants" to supplement his catalogs with a variety of human interest and horticultural articles as well as recent news from his nursery. Not until the September-October issue of 1924 does Farr inform his readers about the move to Womelsdorf. On the *second* page he begins with an announcement in bold print of a once-in-a-generation nursery moving sale. Then he explains the two main reasons behind the move to what he regards as a more desirable location: increasing overhead in the Wyomissing location and isolated fields and office unable to accommodate the increasing traffic from customers coming by automobile. Farr predicts that "thousands of people will see the new nursery to where a dozen now see the present one."

He also favors the location for its close connection with the abutting Conrad Weiser Park, informing readers that "Conrad Weiser is regarded as the George Washington of Berks County" because "[h]is activities in military, political and financial affairs made him easily the most prominent man in early Berks County history." The park in Weiser's honor contains his grave, homestead, and farm buildings. Furthermore, Farr looks forward to cooperating with the park in having a new Dream Garden. Enthusiastically, he writes:

> *What a treat there will be for motorists in years to come. A historic spot devoted to one of the country's pioneers; a beautifully planted collection of the world's better hardy plants, and a hardy plant nursery operating under the most modern and scientific methods and policies.*

The article reveals that some of the nursery had already been moved, that "75,000 peonies, thousands of evergreens, shrubs and shade trees have been lined out since August, 1923," most of these being small or young plants. The plan was "to start the young plants on the new farm and sell all the saleable material from the Wyomissing nursery." Accordingly, the newsletter continues with several lists of plants on sale – such as "Peony Aristocrats," "English Iris," "Superb Peonies" and other hardy perennials – at prices cut 25 to 50 per cent.

Introducing a New Nursery

Farr Nursery Company now completely moved from the back roads of Wyomissing to a William Penn Highway location at Weiser Park, Womelsdorf, Pa.

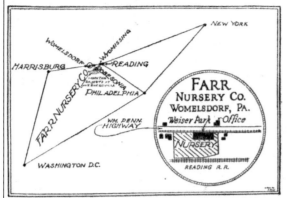

Visitors welcome at Weiser Park. This map for your convenience

The Farr office on the William Penn Highway, Weiser Park, Womelsdorf, Penna.

The Reasons for Moving

A summary of the reasons for moving from Wyomissing, Pa., to Weiser Park, Womelsdorf, Pa., includes (*a*) better soil; (*b*) proximity to farm labor; (*c*) **a thousand times as many motorists will pass the new location as was the case in Wyomissing**; (*d*) the new Weiser Park land-cost is one-fifth that of the Wyomissing location.

How Accomplished

In brief, the major policy which governed development of the new nursery was to sell off the plants at Wyomissing and to grow new crops at Weiser Park. Very few salable plants were moved from Wyomissing to Weiser Park. Most of the trucking was confined to daily transportation of workers and small plants from the Wyomissing frames and propagating-house to the Weiser Park development.

The moving of a nursery is not a simple or an every-day matter, at least not a matter of a few trucks and a few days. Rather, as we have learned, an undertaking which requires years of work and many sleepless nights. We are glad we moved and glad we're through moving.

History of Weiser Park

The Weiser Park location is developed and so named because it is the site of the Conrad Weiser farm. It is one of the oldest farms in Pennsylvania; the original deed from William Penn to Conrad Weiser is in the possession of the Berks County Historical Society at Reading, the county-seat. A reproduction of the bronze tablet visible on the Conrad Weiser home (illustration appearing on page 31), reads as follows:

Home of Conrad Weiser 1729~1760

Churchman, counsellor, soldier, Indian interpreter, agent, diplomat, and first judge of Berks County.

Here were held many conferences with Indian chiefs, missionaries, Colonial governors, and leaders.

Here were reared his children, of whom the eldest daughter, Anna Maria, married Rev. Henry Melchior Muhlenberg, the "Patriarch of the Lutheran Church in America."

Here he died July 13, 1760, and lies buried in the family plot nearby, together with his father, his wife, several children, and a number of friendly Indian chiefs.

He so ably served the Colonies as Indian interpreter and diplomat that he is regarded as the pivotal man who brought the country under Anglo-Saxon versus Latin civilization.

"POSTERITY CANNOT FORGET HIS SERVICES."

PRESIDENT GEORGE WASHINGTON

Accomplishments and Innovations at Weiser Park

Included among the multitude of accomplishments at Weiser Park location are: (*a*) Scientific and comprehensive soil survey and analysis followed by application of lime, fertilizers, and cover crops according to findings; (*b*) construction of a dam and installation of an irrigation system; (*c*) sunken road construction to prevent soil-erosion; (*d*) maintenance of a herd of cattle for the natural fertilizer by-product; (*e*) erection of a new propagating-house; (*f*) construction of concrete propagating-frames; (*g*) methodical and scientific crop-rotation; (*h*) elimination of lesser varieties and concentrated efforts on the remaining better kinds.

Some plants were being discarded anyway because of the new iris and peony rating standards. The "old" Dream Garden plus some shrubs were going to be moved to the Museum grounds. Some plants were simply left in place. Most of the Bertrand H. Farr – Wyomissing Nurseries Co. land, as it turned out, was not actually developed until after World War II. Local residents in the new developments often found a number of mysterious plants just growing wild in yards and vacant lots in the 1950's and beyond.

The accompanying page copied from the nursery catalog of 1927 helps explain Conrad Weiser and the park, but also reveals information more directly related to Farr and the nursery. The four parts to "The Reasons for Moving," as readers will note, avoids the fifth reason having to do with the Wyomissing Development Company's plans. The third reason, in bold face, is probably a true statement, but not really relevant to what had been Farr's mail order business. However, by 1927, for the new owners (and they will be explained in the next chapter) local retail business and landscaping business would largely replace the mail order business; and so this location would hold an advantage over the Wyomissing business with its nursery fields scattered around the area and without any central focus for customers. The fourth reason, having to do with reduced land cost, sounds like a plus. On the other hand, the nursery was now less than half as big.

In his last year Farr spent a lot of time traveling. In the spring of 1924, he paid a short visit to Webster City, something he had occasionally done in the past to visit friends and, in this case, also to see the new plantings on Des Moines Street. In 1922 Farr had shipped a collection of about 70 iris and 18 peony plants to his former home town of Webster City as a gift to the local garden club "to beautify the boulevard flower beds" and, at the same time, to honor his wife, Anna, who was still remembered in the town as a musician and as a member of the Six O'clock Club. The *Daily News* identified some of the plants Farr had sent – peonies such as **Festiva Maxima, Duchesse de Nemours, Francois Rousseau,** and **Edulis Superba;** and irises such as **Quaker Lady, James Boyd, Powhatan, Iris King** and **White Knight.**

A man devoted to the various horticultural organizations of which he was a member or officer, Farr traveled frequently to attend organizational meetings. He earned a reputation as a very collaborative participant in the business meetings and as a very sociable man who just loved to talk with other people about plants. On March 21 he attended the directors meeting of the Iris Society in New York and then its annual meeting and show on May 27 in Washington, D.C. Frank Presby, fellow director and treasurer of the Iris Society, wrote right after Farr's death (and just before his own death) that the two were together in Washington and stayed up talking until one o'clock.

On June 21 – 23 he was in Des Moines, Iowa at the annual Peony Society meeting. Miss Izanne Chamberlain, from the local garden club hosting the Society's meeting, commented later, "I can say without hesitation that [Mr. Farr] was one of the greatest attractions of the meeting as everyone realized that he was an authority not to be disputed and at the same time had such a genial personality that everybody wanted to meet him." Miss Chamberlain, also reported how, at the evening garden party she and the garden club gave for Society members at her home, she and Farr and some other lingering guests stayed up talking in the moonlight until midnight – "a feast of reason and a flow of soul." Farr had visited her on another occasion when he gave a talk to the Des Moines garden club. Earlier, she had purchased 17 varieties of iris and 12 of lilacs from his first catalog in 1908. She knew him and his plants well:

> *Mr. Farr was not a nurseryman in the ordinary sense of the word. This is evident*
> *in all the editorial introductions of his catalogues. He had a great deal of sentiment*
> *and poetic feeling for the things he loved and I believe his love for flowers entirely*
> *overshadowed any monetary interest he had in them.*

A fourth meeting he attended, the date is unreported, was in New York for the Eastern Nurserymen's Association. Farr's last clearly reported trip was back to Boston one more time to attend the annual meeting of the American Rose Society on September 24-25.

After a stroke while he was dressing on Monday, October 6, 1924, and just three days short of his 61st birthday on Saturday, October 11, Bertrand H. Farr died. The next Monday in the Farr home in Wyomissing, funeral services were conducted by the Rev. Dr. Robert Marshall Blackburn from the First Presbyterian Church in Reading, where Farr had been a member. Farr's wife, Anna, and his sister, Mrs. J.O. (Nellie) Crawford of Chicago took Farr's body back to Webster City, Iowa for a funeral service and burial there.

The *Reading Eagle* reported that "Mr. Farr was apparently in the best of health and frequently told his many friends that he never felt better in his life." The day after his stroke he had been scheduled to give a lecture, part of a series of lectures he was giving on flowers to garden clubs. In Webster City, the *Daily News*, in a different vein, said: "Some people give the world railroads and bridges; some keep the books and cure the sick. Bertrand Farr has as important a position as any of these. It was his task to glorify nature and he performed it well."

The "Better Plants" newsletter came out on November 15 as a Special Memorial Issue. Next to an eye-catching photograph of Mrs. Farr near the top of the front page are two blocked-off, brief messages. One is "Our Tribute to Our Chief" from The Farr Organization hailing "his sincerity and idealism, which won for him a host of friends and admirers" and pledging to bring credit to his memory and to assist Mrs. Farr "in the continuation of the hopes and dreams of our late Chief's life work." The lower block, from Anna Farr, is her one sentence about missing "Mr. Farr's genius and guidance" and promising the continuation of the Company's "principles, policies, and ideals."

Below her picture is a column of text announcing her election by the board of directors on November 6 as the new President and describing her previous roles in the business:

> *In the early days, when Mr. Farr was building up the business, Mrs. Farr devoted many long hours to tedious details. She became actively interested in office and field operations, and Mr. Farr sought her counsel in many of his undertakings.*

Otherwise unidentified woman is presumed to be Anna Farr. From Farr's 1915 catalog with caption:
The Mistress of the Garden with an armful of Triomphe du Nord

MRS. BERTRAND H. FARR

Left: Page from 1917 catalog with caption: *Iris, Anna Farr. The chaste beauty of this Iris is difficult to describe. Because of its daintiness and charm, I consider it the gem of my Wyomissing seedlings*
Right: From Memorial Issue of *Better Plants*, 1924

Two other paragraphs emphasize her continued help and enthusiasm after the incorporation and affirm the staff's confidence in her leadership.

Death often has a way of uncovering hidden information, as is the case here; and that information now is about the woman behind the man. In the time between Anna Farr's marriage and this memorial page for her husband, there is almost nothing else about her in the apparently available records. Nothing previous to this very brief article about her has come up about her role in the business or any other role either, except being listed as a music teacher; and the only other photos would seem to be just one, or maybe two, unidentified pictures of her in the catalogs. By the end of 1925, she has sold the business to three of the nursery's managers. Catharine Keiser Reed remembers that Anna Farr also sold her house on Wyomissing Boulevard and lived for a time in an apartment, possibly helped by the Wyomissing textile men. This apartment was at the corner of Penn and Eighth Avenues in the building of their Delta Realty Co., another real estate business these men had. Later her brief obituary in the *Reading Times* for May 7, 1940 reported that she had died the day before in her home at 630 Centre Avenue in Reading, had been a member of the First Presbyterian Church and both the Reading and Wyomissing Woman's Clubs, and would be buried in the Memorial Mausoleum in Wyomissing Hills (another suburb of Reading merged with Wyomissing in 2002).

Inside the "Better Plants" memorial issue are a biographical sketch of Bertrand Farr and photographs of him as a Wyomissing Man and an Iowa Boy and of his office staff and field forces. Also, some tribute letters from a Webster City friend; two different nurseries in Sassenheim, Holland; two American magazine editors; two officers of the American Iris Society; and Farr's catalog publisher. Excerpts from several of these tributes deserve a place here.

From John Wister, the Iris Society president: "Mr. Farr has done much for the iris in America, for it is due to him, more than to any other one person or group of persons, that the iris has attained its present popularity here." And, "[His] interest in the Iris was, however, only a small part of his love for all hardy plants, and all American gardeners owe him a great debt for his work in making popular and available many hitherto unknown, or little known plants."

From Madison Cooper, Editor of *The Flower Grower*: "Bertrand H. Farr helped mightily to make the world a better place in which to live."

From R.S. Sturtevant, Iris Society secretary: "He was not one of these secretive gardeners, sure of the merit of their work and jealous of their methods, but rather a seeker after the best in life and in gardens, eager to share with and learn from others."

Undoubtedly there were many, many other letters coming in from around the country and the world, but only a few of them could be selected for this slender nursery newsletter; and, except for just a few left in Womelsdorf, they have been lost.

Letters written to Farr when he was alive might actually serve even better as tributes to him, letters from his customers. Scattered at the bottoms of pages in a few of his catalogs and selected, of course, by Farr as testimonials to the quality of his business, these letters provide another revealing vocabulary for measuring the man, letters from places like Sulligent, Alabama; Danville, Illinois; Elginton, Ontario; Manila, Philippine Islands; and Napier, New Zealand.

From Walter P. Hull, Kansas: "[The] order went to you because I wanted to be sure of getting true varieties; the sad mixture I have received from some other sources has cured me for all time of patronizing the 'cheap' class of plantsmen."

From R.E. Smith, New York: "The roots came to me in first-class shape and I do not hesitate to say that they were the finest lot of roots that I have seen in a long time."

From Jno. B. Simmons, Wisconsin: "I take pleasure in saying to you that [your plants] are in all respects the *best* lot I have ever received from any nurseryman."

From Mrs. D.R. Kerr, Pennsylvania: "The peonies, phlox and iris were received in good time and in excellent condition. I am quite sure I have never received better stock than you sent me, and the price was very moderate."

And, finally, a beautifully-lettered tribute written to Anna Farr from a customer in Williamsport, Pennsylvania. Bryson Hines, a retired Pennsylvania Railroad man, writes about his appreciation for the four-page letter Farr wrote to advise him about taking up gardening and assisting him with establishing a large collection of plants. He writes, "Mr. Farr was first of all a beauty enthusiast and secondarily a business man." and "I regard Bertrand H. Farr as one of the noblest men I have ever met in a lifetime of almost seventy years."

Undated photo of Bertrand H. Farr in Farr Nursery Co. Collection.

Overlooking the Farr Display Garden, which is replete with varieties, novel arrangements, and ideas for convenient stu[dy] and enjoyment by visitors. The garden house permits us to serve friends and customers quickly; the contents include glasswa[re], pottery, and a general assortment of supplies.

Top: photo from the 1930 Farr Nursery Co. catalog showing the William Penn Highway on left, new Display Garden in center, and new nursery fields on upper right

Opposite page: From the 1930 Farr Nursery Co. catalog

Chapter 9

The After Years

effloresce

to burst forth or become manifest as of flowering

—Webster's New International Dictionary

he successors to Bertrand Farr, and to Anna Farr, were men whom Farr had hired in the early 1920's to help manage the office and the nursery sides of the business and who bought the company from Anna Farr on September 18, 1925 for $42,516.42. Dividing the ownership equally were the nurserymen Lester W. Needham, President, and Charles M. Boardman, Vice-President, and businessman Harold G. Seyler, Treasurer. Boardman, living nearby in Sinking Spring, and Needham and Seyler, both living

Ownership and Management of Farr Nursery Company

Presented in the Belief That People Like to Know with Whom They Are Dealing

L. W. Needham, *President*

One-third owner, Manager of Nursery Production and Operations. Employed by the late Mr. Farr in 1922.

C. M. Boardman, *Vice-President*

One-third owner, Manager of Landscape Department and Local Sales. Employed by the late Mr. Farr in 1923.

H. G. Seyler, *Treasurer*

One-third owner, Manager of Office and Mail Order Department. Employed by the late Mr. Farr in 1920.

Photo dated 1930 in the Farr Nursery collection with "Display Garden" and signs of thriving business

in Holland Square in Wyomissing, soon moved to Womelsdorf to complete the transfer of the business from Wyomissing by 1927. Although the legal name remained as before, Bertrand H. Farr – Wyomissing Nurseries Company, the public name became Farr Nursery Company and later, in accord with the changing emphasis of the business, Farr Nursery and Landscape Company.

This changing emphasis, which Farr himself had helped to initiate, led to the gradual decline of the plants for which Farr had been most famous, especially the iris and the peony. Symbolic of this change, the "Better Plants by Farr" catalogs now had the iris and peony sections at the end. Taking over their former place at the beginning were Evergreens, Shade and Woodland Trees, and Deciduous Flowering Shrubs. The new owners clearly wanted to take advantage, too, of their new location on the William Penn Highway, where, as announced on the first page of the 1930 catalog, "50,000 people pass on one busy Sunday or holiday, and 5,000 critical visitors are received on one day during the bloom season." With that amazing volume of traffic, emphasis shifted heavily toward local sales and services and away from mail order. By 1930, 800 different plants had been discarded. The new owners were not interested in owning the largest collections of various plants, as they indicated in announcing, for example, that 140 varieties of phlox had been reduced to 50 and 130 lilacs to 50.

The Farr legacy in Womelsdorf, for any extended time, rested mainly with the daylilies and the contract with Arlow Stout in New York. The new owners – and it was especially Harold Seyler who became the steady link with Stout – honored the arrangement Bertrand Farr had made in the early 1920's. By 1930 the process of Stout's sending his hybrid daylilies to Womelsdorf for the Farr nurserymen to propagate and test had resulted in four Arlow Stout introductions: **Cinnibar, Mikado, Vesta,** and **Wau-Bun.** Three of Bertrand Farr's hybrids also were listed at 75 cents each: **Golconda, Mandarin,** and **Ophir.** In 1931, it should be said, **Ophir** won an "Award of Merit" from the Royal Horticultural Society and is still a popular daylily.

In New York, Stout is reported to have made around 50,000 daylily crosses by the time he retired in 1948. In Womelsdorf, according to a 1957 letter from Harold Seyler to the New York Botanical Garden, the Farr Nursery had introduced to the national trade 83 successful daylilies and had 12 more waiting to be introduced from Stout's transfer to the Farr Nursery of his daylily collection when he retired. Even as late as 1955, in his retirement and just two years before he died, Stout came to Womelsdorf to help evaluate and select the daylilies for introduction. In 1952 the Farr Nursery issued a 15-page catalog devoted to "Dr. Stout's Hybrid Daylilies" and containing detailed listings of 54 of them, all priced variously for three dollars or less and the whole collection for $69.95.

In 1946 the American Hemerocallis Society was founded, and in 1950 the Society created the Bertrand Farr Silver Medal to be awarded to a member for outstanding results in daylily hybridizing. The first award went to Arlow B. Stout. The same year the Society also established the Arlow Stout Silver Medal to be awarded for the best new daylily. Today the Society is divided into 15 regional associations across America and Canada, and each region includes numerous local associations totaling almost 200. The combined membership is around 10,000. According to registrar Gretchen Baxter there currently are 61,384 registered daylilies, and the number keeps growing. Annual registrations during the past several years have averaged around 2,400. Many of these daylilies can be viewed at the 325 display gardens society members have created.

The Bertrand Farr name lives on in two ways connected with the daylily. In 1941 the Farr Nursery introduced the **Bertrand Farr** daylily, named by Stout from a cross he had made between **Patricia** and **Charmaine;** and Farr's namesake is still grown. The other way, of course, is that the Farr medal has been awarded annually since 1950. If one does a "Bertrand Farr" search on the worldwide web, about 80 per cent of the results will appear for the individual medal winners.

Unfortunately, in this centennial year of the first Farr catalog of 1908, the Farr Nursery and Landscape Company in Womelsdorf is going out of business. The land is for sale, and the nursery stock is quite bare. The current owner, Richard Hawk, plans to continue working as a landscape consultant, but without any nursery.

Bertrand Farr's hope to recreate his own new Dream Garden in Womelsdorf faded with his death. However, the new owners did create a Farr Display Garden near the highway, as advertised in their 1930 catalog, "replete with varieties, novel arrangements, and ideas for convenient study and enjoyment by visitors." One photograph in this catalog shows a curved bed of tulips and a caption saying the garden has "30,000 Tulips in 168 varieties." Later Farr Nursery catalogs reflect the diminishing emphasis on irises but continued numbers of select peony and lilac varieties.

In Wyomissing, Farr's Dream Garden was being prepared for moving and new use at the Reading Public Museum. In the spring after Farr's death, on April 5, 1925 the headlines in the *Reading Tribune* announced:

ROOT PRUNING STARTS AS FIRST OPERATION
TOWARD ESTABLISHING OF FARR MEMORIAL ARBORETUM
AT GROUNDS OF READING MUSEUM

Trees and Shrubs Worth $10,000 Will Be Given, Starting Next Fall

Gift Is Fulfillment of Wish That Wyomissing Genius Had Uttered

The article explained that the Wyomissing Development Company had men pruning the tap roots of the many trees and shrubs Farr had donated so that fibrous roots would develop to keep the trees and shrubs alive when transplanted. Lester Needham, from the Farr Nursery, was collaborating with the town planner John Nolen in planning for the arrangement of the nursery materials, which Needham estimated had a value of $10,000.

Most of the rest of the article detailed why John J. Greene, the *Tribune* Sunday Editor, felt that figure "surely is not too high." Among Farr's donations were 50 species of evergreens, including some rare Asian ones and cedars of Lebanon; 30 some species of mock orange; 15 kinds of Oriental magnolias; 15 kinds of Japanese cherry trees; 25 of crabapples, some from the Arnold Arboretum; a rare collection of Japanese tree peonies; and 100 varieties of lilacs.

A month earlier a shorter report in the *Reading Times* stated that all these donations amounted to between 400 and 500 varieties for a total of about 1,500 plants. Some of the larger trees were to be moved in the fall, some of the smaller plants in the current spring, but the rest in the following year. The tree removal was to be done by means of an "underground derrick which gently releases the roots from the earth."

In 1927 the first of a long tradition of Lilac Sundays was held featuring 120 varieties of lilacs from Farr's collection. Groundbreaking for the museum building and landscaping had begun in 1925. The museum building itself would not be fully opened to the public until 1928; but in 1927, with the building opened on Sundays and enough plants in place, the Reading School Board felt comfortable inviting the public to this first lilac event. An estimated 15,000 to 20,000 attended the event despite a rainy afternoon.

By 1928 the *Reading Times* was announcing the second annual event, this time with 150 lilac varieties from Farr's garden. The article states that the museum gardeners were still busy transplanting "the large collection of lilacs, iris, shrubs and trees," positioning them near the museum building and along walkways in flower beds and at "advantageous points" and preparing for the 15,000 visitors expected the next Sunday. The article also makes special mention of the source of the lilac varieties, especially from the Lemoine nurseries, and names some of the lilacs visitors would be enjoying: **President Poincaire, President Fallieres, Leon Gambetta, Siebold, Ludwig Spathe, Miss Ellen Willmott, and Mme. Casimir Perier.**

According to a museum report, the tradition of Lilac Sunday continued for 40 years until

1967. Gone now are the lilacs and most of the rest of Farr's donations, but still growing in the arboretum, through which the Wyomissing Creek flows, are some of his hardy trees.

It should be mentioned, however, that the Reading Public Museum, an accredited museum, has had much to manage. It is unusual for its wide-ranging natural history collections (50,000 butterflies to many thousands of mammals and birds to 25,000 minerals), world civilization galleries (Egyptian mummy to Greek "Krater" vases to Inca textiles and Chinese porcelain), and art collections (Brueghel to Degas to Wyeth and Pennsylvania-German antiques). On the grounds of the arboretum, the museum operates a planetarium. The museum staff mounts frequent special exhibits and hosts a wide variety of educational programs for schools and the community. Unusual also for having been both owned by and under the administration of the Reading School Department until 1992, the museum is now administered by a private, non-profit foundation but is still owned by the school department.

This transfer of administration has resulted in some better fundraising capabilities and increased attention to the museum's arboretum, which had been largely kept "wild" for many years. Still without an employed gardener, the arboretum is tended by groups of volunteer enthusiasts and master gardeners. However, recently the museum has been planning for a major renovation of the arboretum and will be embarking on what is likely to be a fifteen-year project.

As a part of this project, the arboretum committee will be working to establish an iris garden in honor of Bertrand Farr, using some of his historic irises and being assisted in the creation of this garden by members of the American Iris and the Historic Iris Preservation Societies.

Otherwise, only faint traces of the Farr presence in his home area remain. The Iris Club, the eating club established by the Wyomissing textile and development men and named in honor of Farr, is no longer operating and is practically an abandoned building. As mentioned earlier, the former Farr nursery land bought by the Wyomissing Development Company partners Ferdinand Thun and Irvin Impink in Wyomissing and the 18th Ward of Reading, an area to be developed as Wyomissing Park and planned by John Nolen, was not developed until after World War II. By that time the development company had gone out of business, the land was in the hands of Ferdinand Thun's heirs, and, as various contractors began building houses, the Borough of Wyomissing town engineer Bob Seidel named the initial streets, setting the pattern for the whole series of streets named after birds. The Farr nursery area then became known as "Birdland" with streets such as Thrush Road, Cardinal Place, and Bluebird Drive. At what approximately was the eastern boundary of the fields Farr bought in 1916, there is a Farr Road and its adjoining Farr Place loop.

MAY 15 LILAC SUNDAY AT READING PUBLIC MUSEUM AND ART GALLERY

PARK SURROUNDING BUILDING RAPIDLY BECOMING THE FOREMOST SHOWPLACE IN READING — HUNDREDS OF TREES, SHRUBS AND FLOWERING PLANTS BEING SET OUT EACH WEEK

Transporting Trees and Large Plants.

From *Reading Eagle,* May 8, 1927

Reading Public Museum, as it looked in 1936 after landscaping

Farr's name lived on, for a time, when in 1928 the American Peony Society established a Farr Memorial Medal, which was first awarded to James Boyd for editing *The Manual of the American Peony Society,* published that year. Afterward, it was usually awarded for the best or "grand champion" peony more or less regularly until 1985. Curiously, that same year when Farr's medal award was dropped, a letter from a citizen in Webster City was printed in the Society's *Bulletin* about the gift of plants Farr had made to Webster City in 1922. Through neglect, the growth of weeds, and the encroachment by veterans organizations with their "cannon, boulders, bronze plaques, etc." most of the plants had disappeared. Two peony plants, however, probably **Festiva Maxima,** had survived for 63 years; and this good citizen was cutting weeds and taking seeds to save the plants.

*M*uch more significant, obviously, than medals or street names, Farr's legacy has been what his colleagues in the horticultural world began to anticipate at his death, especially affirmed in the praise that came from Iris Society president John Wister about the importance of Farr's pioneering work with many different hardy plants, not just the iris, and its effect in stimulating the popularity of these plants in America. Through his efforts in importing, collecting, growing, hybridizing, introducing, identifying, collaborating, lecturing, and dreaming, Farr inspired other nurserymen and his customers and helped to create an efflorescence in American horticulture.

This flowering outburst, already suggested earlier in the daylily world, is further demonstrated in the surge of interest in the iris and peony and the growth of their two societies. Both the American Iris and the American Peony Society serve as umbrellas for many American and Canadian gardeners and nurserymen who belong to affiliated regional, state, or city societies, all pursuing their love of growing irises or peonies (or both), sharing information, holding exhibits, competing for new and better cultivars, registering the new ones, inviting members and others to their display gardens and, in many ways, helping the general public to learn about, appreciate and grow these hardy perennials. These societies take very seriously the importance of the tradition that Bertrand Farr helped to establish in the early 1900's – the proper identification and registration of each plant and the obligation of nurseries to sell their plants "true to name."

Harvey Buchite, a Minnesota nurseryman and current president of the American Peony Society, bemoans the way this tradition is sometimes ignored so that the implied contract between seller and buyer about plant identity is violated. Of course, since Farr's day many more new plants are introduced per year, making the registration and identification process that much more difficult. Reiner Jakubowski, the current registrar for the Peony Society reports that since 1974 the Society has registered 1,488 new peonies. Accordingly, the registrar and the society help to avoid what Farr spent part of six summers at Cornell to correct. The Society has about 900 members and nine regional associations from Maine to the Pacific Northwest.

By comparison with the American Iris Society, the Peony Society prides itself in being a cosy "family," while the irisarians are a complex of "nations." With a membership of around 5,600, the American Iris Society shelters 24 regional societies and 173 local societies. In addition to all these "general iris" groups, there are nine specialized societies like the Dwarf Iris, the Reblooming, the Siberian, and the Historic Iris Preservation Societies.

According to registrars Mike and Anne Lowe, there are currently over 50,000 registered irises. During the past several years, they have registered over 1,000 new hybrid irises each year. Nursery growers in America and other countries, eager to produce new irises to sell, recently have been pushing these numbers well over 1,000.

The Historic Iris Preservation Society (HIPS) is the organization most important for preserving the Bertrand Farr legacy because the members are the individual gardeners and nurseries still growing, preserving, displaying and maintaining records of many of the irises Farr hybridized and introduced. Organized in 1989, HIPS now has about 650 members across the

United States and Canada, individual gardeners and commercial growers who include historic irises (those irises introduced more than 30 years ago) in their gardens. Of the over 30,000 historic irises, the HIPS data base reveals that 3,857 of them are still grown. The society's biannual journal and its comprehensive website provide information about display gardens, commercial sources and member-donated rhizome sales as well as the historic iris data base, full-color photos of historic irises, and news and articles of organizational interest. One of these articles, in the spring 2003 issue of the HIPS journal *ROOTS* by Anne Lowe, the first president of HIPS, featured the life and work of Bertrand Farr.

Of the 3,857 historic irises still grown (out of the over 30, 000 historic irises) at least 15 (and perhaps others not yet on the data base) of Farr's irises are still grown and available for viewing, trading or buying: **Apache, Blue Jay, Japanesque, Juniata, Mount Penn, Mildred Presby, Navajo, Nokomis, Pocahontas, Quaker Lady, Red Cloud, Rose Unique, Sea-Gull, Seminole** and **Wyomissing.**

Some of these irises can be viewed at public gardens in the East – the Center for Historic Plants at Jefferson's Monticello in Charlottesville, Virginia; the newly restored garden at the Frederick Law Olmsted National Historic Site in Brookline, Massachusetts; and at the nearby Longfellow National Historic Site in Cambridge. The richest collection of historic irises in a public garden is in Upper Montclair, New Jersey in the Presby Memorial Iris Garden. Begun in 1927 in honor of Frank Presby by his fellow townspeople, the garden now displays 1,500 historic irises in addition to 1,000 later ones, most of which were donated originally by local people who admired Frank Presby for his community leadership, his help in founding the American Iris Society, and his own enthusiasm for growing irises. Later additions have gradually come in from all over the country. One of the featured irises displayed there is **Mildred Presby,** specially grown by Bertrand Farr and selected by Presby to honor his older daughter during one of his visits with Farr in Wyomissing. Thirteen other Farr irises are on display in this iris garden, which attracts thousands of visitors each year.

In addition to these four gardens, HIPS lists about 40 other official Display Gardens from New York to California featuring from 100 to as many as 1,600 historic irises, not many of Farr's irises, though, since they have to compete today with all the thousands of other historic irises.

However, one stalwart Farr iris, one of his earliest introductions, has competed well – **Quaker Lady.** The first president of the Iris Society, John Wister, wrote in 1924: "Of all the dainty and charming irises nothing can surpass Quaker Lady with its many varied hues of smoky lavender, bronze, purple, fawn, and old gold all mixed together." A recent president of the Iris Society, Clarence Mahan, in his book *Classic Irises and the Men and Women Who Created Them* titles his chapter on Bertrand Farr "Quaker Lady, Bertrand Farr, and a Pennsylvania Legacy" and calls **Quaker Lady** "[Farr's] most famous iris." Mahan, agreeing with Wister, describes this iris as "that rarity of irises, a cultivar that is both elegant and pretty – not majestically beautiful – but pretty. It is, in brief, a charming iris." Many historic iris growers today also agree; for, in a recent HIPS survey of the most commonly grown historic irises, **Quaker Lady** ranked fifteenth.

Quaker Lady and Farr's other historic irises represent important parts of the iris knowledge base, something the American Iris Society was concerned with after Farr's death. On March 15, 1928 a letter went out to AIS members from the Farr Memorial Library Committee soliciting contributions for "one or more Traveling Libraries as a memorial to the late Bertrand H. Farr." The idea was to purchase all books, magazines, and any other publications devoted to the iris and to make them available around America. The idea was fully realized almost immediately. Anner Whitehead, a former Iris Society administrative officer, has directed attention to AIS *Bulletin* No. 30 of January 1929 giving library committee chairman Richardson Wright's report that almost $900 was in the account, iris publications had been purchased for three traveling libraries, three special shipping cartons built, and the country divided into three regions for garden clubs to borrow a Farr Library for one month at a time. This circulation of "Iris lore" for both amateurs and experts enabled, in Wright's words, AIS's "unique way [in] carrying on the aspiration of him in whose memory it has been established. 'Iris everywhere and better Iris every year' was the ideal of Bertrand H. Farr."

Important and famous as Bertrand Farr was for irises and peonies and daylilies, his most significant legacy is as a Hardy Plant Nurseryman. Very quickly he turned his hobby not so much into a business (as he liked to assert), but rather into a profession. In mid-life he found his principal calling and, without formal training, became an expert in horticulture. He issued catalogs, and he made them both informative and poetic. He sold plants, and he was always most interested, as he wrote in the beginning of his first catalog, in surrounding himself with beautiful flowers and sharing them with his many visitors.

Born on a mountain side in Vermont, raised on the prairie in the middle of Iowa, hoping to become a piano prodigy in Boston, inspired by the Hovey & Co. nursery in Cambridge, and moving to his new home in the new suburb of Wyomissing, Bertrand Farr became a leading citizen of the horticultural world, helping to define that world and to expand that world for any others who wanted to follow him and have their own Dream Gardens.

As we leave Bertrand Farr and his life story, let his own words, from the end of his Introduction to his Sixth Edition Catalog for the Season of 1918, speak:

> *I want to express my keen appreciation of the generous patronage which has made all of this [Dream Garden collection] possible, which in a measure makes it partly yours, and you may at all times feel assured that you will be welcome when you come.*

> *Have you ever heard the ringing*
> *Of the bobolink's sweet singing*
> *In some meadow far away?*
> *When the world , with all its sadness,*
> *Seems to slowly drift away,*
> *As you drink in joy and gladness*
> *With the balmy breath of May.*
> *So you bridge life's years of struggle*
> *On the bobolink's sweet strain,*
> *To the golden years of childhood,*
> *And you are a boy again.*

Appendix

Appendix

Bertrand Farr's mid-life adventures into the world of hardy plants had many dimensions, many horticultural ones obviously, but also financial ones; and it is the financial side of Farr's 25(or so)-year enterprise that would be fascinating to understand. However, the only financial records remaining in the Womelsdorf office (in a cardboard carton along with other assorted papers and photographs) were statements from 1916 to 1924 – balance sheets and income statements for each year, all apparently typed up at about the same time, presumably but not conclusively, from the earlier original statements compiled each year. Consequently, I am not able to vouch for the reliability of these records given the form they are in and the lack of any kind of verification.

Nevertheless, I am including the records in the following appendix for readers to interpret as they wish. To make these records more manageable and easier to compare, an accountant friend of mine has transferred the numbers from the 18 individual sheets into Excel format. He made only slight adjustments from the typed statements in combining minor categories.

If all these numbers are reliable, there is still one large problem in interpreting them. We have no way to know how Farr valued his inventory at the beginning and end of each year, and those inventory numbers play a considerable role in determining profit or loss. Of course, the even bigger set of mysteries concerns Farr's financial and nursery management history from the years *before* 1916, from the years when he began growing plants in the late 1890's in Wyomissing, importing plants on a large scale, leasing fields, and gradually having to deal with the many complications of running his nursery.

126

It is easy to overlook those complications. Beyond the usual weather problems all farmers and nurserymen must face, unlike the farmers, who normally sell all their products each season, nurserymen like Farr must keep a steady inventory of the plants they don't sell and all the ones that are still in process of maturing. Even worse, in striving for new hybrids (like irises) Farr often discarded thousands of plants deemed unworthy. In Farr's case again, he obviously did not follow recommended current business practice for nurseries to grow and sell many plants of only a few varieties – better ten top varieties, 10,000 each, than 100 varieties, 100 each.

Although it certainly appears that Farr had many satisfied mail-order customers, running a mail-order nursery is fraught with the complications and expenses of handling orders, timing and pulling of the plants, providing packaging materials, packing the plants and bare roots, mailing everything safely, advertising to a widely scattered national market while also trying to serve a mostly-local landscaping market. It is not surprising that Farr's nursery was not a very profitable business, judging from these business records

In any case, for the record, here they are. And, for the reader's interest, I am also including other exhibits related to Bertrand Farr and his world.

Bertrand H. Farr—Wyomissing Nurseries Co.
Profit & Loss & Accumulated Surplus

	1916	1917	1918	1919
Sales				
Nursery Stock	46,481.28	60,871.39	40,318.03	78,209.67
Bulbs	3,798.39	4,239.88	4,320.25	6,658.15
	50,279.67	65,111.27	44,638.28	84,867.82
Less: Discounts	1,290.44	2,274.22		192.71
Net Sales	48,989.23	62,837.05	44,638.28	84,675.11
Cost of Sales				
Inventory at beginning	76,465.00	102,296.75	116,640.01	127,299.89
Purchases	18,671.89	23,242.08	12,154.43	38,359.39
Freight	5,400.00	-		
Total	100,536.89	125,538.83	128,794.44	165,659.28
Less: Inventory at end	102,296.75	116,640.01	130,299.89	141,886.42
Cost of Sales	(1,759.86)	8,898.82	(1,505.45)	23,772.86
Gross Profit On Sales	50,749.09	53,938.23	46,143.73	60,902.25
Expenses				
Advertising-Cat & Postage	8,541.50	8,101.44	2,345.23	4,309.39
-Magazine	-	4,008.55	2,777.09	4,830.46
-Mail & other				
Organization expens	869.82			
Officers' salaries	3,625.00	3,942.30	4,645.20	4,519.00
Wages	20,288.25	27,196.11	21,849.71	33,137.75
Shipping & rel exps	488.27	199.23	62.52	529.88
Office supplies & exp	1,371.59	2,098.96	1,280.10	1,608.42
Automobile expense	872.36	1,629.26	1,566.32	2,051.99
Stable expense	1,072.00	1,032.14	457.63	315.99
Nurseries expense	2,659.69	2,068.52	2,264.26	5,009.95
Farm expenses				1,840.25
Heat & light	-	411.49	502.48	558.49
Interest & discount	920.41	1,567.19	2,619.01	2,746.67
Rent	97.92	323.45	202.52	
Taxes	156.65	1,000.55	1,672.59	1,346.75
Insurance	181.75	153.69	347.17	536.07
Real estate expense				
Bad debts		282.00	42.57	300.00
Depreciation		512.61	509.95	486.63
Total expenses	41,145.21	54,527.49	43,144.35	64,127.79
	9,603.88	(589.26)	2,999.38	(3,225.54)
Other income	380.87	2,066.58	2,228.05	1,560.64
Profit on real estate				
NET PROFIT (LOSS)	9,984.75	1,477.32	5,227.43	(1,664.90)
Surplus(Deficit),At Beginning	-	9,984.75	6,303.90	11,504.33
Dividends paid	-	(5,158.17)		
Adjustment to balance			(27.00)	(398.32)
Surplus (Deficit), At End	9,984.75	6,303.90	11,504.33	9,441.11

1920	1921	1922	1923	1924
75,827.62	95,074.90	92,375.32	104,765.17	112,263.13
8,625.28	6,432.42	7,328.72	10,909.75	11,416.61
84,452.90	101,507.32	99,704.04	115,674.92	123,679.74
47.70				
84,405.20	101,507.32	99,704.04	115,674.92	123,679.74
141,886.42	119,237.41	104,668.97	87,948.05	89,324.68
9,468.18	21,193.46	33,260.62	19,655.69	21,930.63
151,354.60	140,430.87	137,929.59	107,603.74	111,255.31
119,237.41	104,668.97	87,948.05	89,324.68	84,137.52
32,117.19	35,761.90	49,981.54	18,279.06	27,117.79
52,288.01	65,745.42	49,722.50	97,395.86	96,561.95
7,667.50	4,554.30	7,843.35	1,460.47	6,363.77
2,968.40	4,453.74	6,362.35	3,932.51	2,633.10
178.78	1,204.15	2,856.27	7,100.48	4,383.18
4,812.50	5,240.00	5,980.00	6,260.00	6,490.00
41,657.40	42,052.88	43,062.82	58,277.89	53,146.33
566.47	571.32	268.81	441.77	366.77
3,690.60	3,526.07	3,691.35	3,227.89	3,718.06
1,968.81	2,517.22	3,422.53	3,167.56	2,791.54
1,000.61	775.03	298.96	371.44	315.86
5,072.88	5,934.35	6,391.51	3,671.86	5,490.48
1,855.25	252.06			
480.39	838.36	598.08	1,072.39	323.47
2,948.15	2,690.14	1,030.94	1,354.27	2,089.28
	101.50	1,198.53	405.85	147.00
1,318.46	2,253.84	1,278.78	3,105.81	1,768.36
515.40	554.73	758.72	660.67	1,100.51
	2,277.72	1,680.42	297.62	135.25
267.48	361.73	834.02	920.18	1,925.02
870.00	1,310.22	2,250.00	1,062.32	1,793.72
77,839.08	81,469.36	89,807.44	96,790.98	94,981.70
(25,551.07)	(15,723.94)	(40,084.94)	604.88	1,580.25
2,172.92	2,283.26	2,438.65	1482.89	1,024.81
	17,252.41	41,989.44		
23,378.15)	3,811.73	4,343.15	2,087.77	2,605.06
9,441.11	(13,937.04)	(10,125.31)	(5,802.16)	(4,246.72)
		(20.00)	(532.33)	5,112.37
(13,937.04)	(10,125.31)	(5,802.16)	(4,246.72)	3,470.71

Bertrand H. Farr—Wyomissing Nurseries Co.
Balance Sheets

	1916	1917	1918
ASSETS			
Cash in bank	5,846.01	18.62	1,107.21
Cash on Hand	35.00	10.30	35.00
Bills receivable	-	11,781.20	7,344.85
Accounts receivable (Net of res.for ba/ds)	3,570.66	3,311.67	7,137.57
Farm products	-	1,040.00	576.25
Inventory	102,296.75	116,640.01	130,299.89
B H Farr			
Real estate	86,820.55	87,151.08	87,151.08
Auto equipment, net of depreciation	499.95	300.00	1,175.17
Stable equipment, net of depreciation	533.50	750.00	636.50
Nursuries equipment	802.40	2,514.75	2,951.94
Office equipment, net of depreciation	894.70	1,002.20	884.30
Deferred charges (Accruals)	536.85	620.37	2,003.36
Options on real estate	-	-	-
Investment	-	-	-
Salaries reserve & reserve fund	-	-	-
TOTAL ASSETS	201,836.37	225,140.20	241,303.12
LIABILITIES & CAPITAL			
Bills payable	14,000.00	13,500.00	33,850.00
Accounts payable	3,294.05	9,266.42	4,127.31
Notes Payable	-	-	
Mortgages payable	38,315.00	36,650.00	36,650.00
Bills receivable - discounted	-	11,781.20	7,000.00
B H Farr			
Accruals & other liabilities	708.24	638.68	1,171.48
Total Liabilities	56,317.29	71,836.30	82,798.79
Capital			
Capital stock	70,000.00	70,000.00	70,000.00
Preferred stock	65,500.00	77,000.00	77,000.00
Surplus (Deficit)	4,826.58	6,303.90	11,504.33
Dividends declared	5,192.50	-	-
Total Capital	145,519.08	153,303.90	158,504.33
TOTAL LIABILITIES & CAPITAL	201,836.37	225,140.20	241,303.12

1919	1920	1921	1922	1923	1924
686.91	246.64	1,153.16	621.68	724.30	1,002.55
1.36	17.27	97.20	46.79	75.97	33.73
-	-	75.00	275.00	75.00	75.00
9,711.11	4,174.38	9,991.90	10,712.32	5,183.05	6,843.89
289.05	262.06	-	-	-	-
141,886.42	119,237.41	104,668.97	87,948.05	89,324.68	84,137.52
	121.59	740.79	1,968.57	1,642.06	2,516.42
78,803.46	79,877.36	65,881.89	13,729.61	15,729.61	31,911.37
958.54	513.54	2,021.93	1,521.44	1,981.80	985.72
586.50	476.50	1,246.50	1,046.50	941.85	879.54
2,796.94	2,681.80	3,112.52	4,765.86	4,777.66	1,848.01
942.41	867.41	779.19	2,009.19	1,859.57	2,012.28
1,285.59	3,522.00	-	-	-	-
6,347.62	6,347.62	-	-	-	-
-	-	-	36.30	36.30	36.30
-	-	-	-	-	-
244,295.91	218,345.58	189,769.05	124,681.31	122,351.85	132,282.33
			-	-	-
12,600.56	3,875.35	13,002.00	18,085.39	13,154.33	2,670.98
37,937.90	44,657.27	11,142.36	16,898.08	17,944.24	18,637.40
36,650.00	36,650.00	28,650.00	3,000.00	3,000.00	15,000.00
-	-	-	-	-	-
566.34	-	-	-	-	-
-	-	-	-	-	3.24
87,754.80	85,182.62	52,794.36	37,983.47	34,098.57	36,311.62
70,000.00	70,000.00	70,000.00	70,000.00	70,000.00	70,000.00
77,100.00	77,100.00	77,100.00	22,500.00	22,500.00	22,500.00
9,441.11	(13,937.04)	(10,125.31)	(5,802.16)	(4,246.72)	3,470.71
-	-	-	-	-	-
156,541.11	133,162.96	136,974.69	86,697.84	88,253.28	95,970.71
244,295.91	218,345.58	189,769.05	124,681.31	122,351.85	132,282.33

Charles M. Hovey, president of the Massachusetts Horticultural Society, 1863-66;
editor of *Magazine of Horticulture*,1834-68; and principal owner of Hovey & Co.'s Cambridge Nurseries,
where Bertrand Farr spent much time while a student at the New England Conservatory of Music, 1883-85

THE *Second Horticultural Hall, Tremont Street*

Massachusetts Horticultural Society library and headquarters, built in 1865, while Charles Hovey was president

PRICE LIST

OF

Choice

Seedling Pæonies

ORIGINATED BY

H. A. TERRY

FLORA GARDEN NURSERY

The proprietor of this Nursery has been growing these Seedling Pæonies for nearly forty years, and has succeeded in producing some very fine varieties, as the following list will show. These flowers are so very hardy, so intensely beautiful and showy, and so easily grown, that every person should have a collection of them. This collection of Seedling Pæonies is considered the best in the United States. Pæonies when dormant will stand much exposure, and can be shipped long distances without injury. They are never attacked by any insect, animal or disease; nor do the plants require protection during the winter, as they are the most hardy and showy of all the garden flowers. The prices are made so low that everyone can afford to have a good assortment of them. All stock is warranted true to name; they can be planted fall or spring, but fall is considered best. Not less than five of one variety at these prices, but to the trade a heavy discount. Price 25c each, except those noted. Those marked with a star will not be for sale until autumn of 1906.

Terms: Cash before shipment unless otherwise agreed upon.

Reference: First National Bank, Council Bluffs.

PRICE LIST FREE ON APPLICATION. ADDRESS

H. A. TERRY ,. CRESCENT, IOWA

Cover of 1906 catalog of H.A. Terry, from whom Bertrand Farr purchased some of his first peonies

THE ROYAL HORTICULTURAL ESTABLISHMENT · LANGPORT · SOMERSET ·

KELWAYS JUBILEE GREETS

THE NEW CENTURY

Two pages from 1901 *Manual* of Kelway & Son, from whom Bertrand Farr purchased some of his first peonies

JANUARY 1st, 1901.

William Kelway.

THE NINETEENTH CENTURY has vanished, her floral garlands besmirched by the smoke of war. We greet the dawn of the Twentieth Century as a herald of peace and bid Flora meet her with hands full of the best and sweetest she has to offer. May the victories of peace be greater than those of war, and may Horticulture, the purest and most peaceful of the arts, flourish exceedingly.

THE FIRST YEAR OF THE NEW CENTURY is the FIFTIETH in the existence of our firm. It is our Jubilee, and this is our Jubilee Number. We trust that we may have extended to us at least as large a share of patronage and recommendation, and of forbearance for our shortcomings, during the years to come as in the fifty which have been completed.

OUR EFFORTS TO SUPPLY THE BEST PLANTS AND SEEDS FOR THE GARDEN, and a reliable and helpful handbook to their purchase and culture, have met with what we can only designate as extraordinary signs of appreciation in the orders and letters of approval received. For the last few years we have annually intimated the necessity for a large increase in the number of copies which we publish of the Manual; in 1900, the increase was 50 per cent.; this

A 2

year we are under the pleasant obligation of printing 25 per cent. more copies than in 1900, and we have, as will be noticed, made many additions to its attractiveness. We are daily informed from far and wide that Kelway's Manual stands at the head of books of its kind and is unique in treatment and usefulness, and as these are ends we set out to attain we are extremely gratified and encouraged to proceed; the contents are an evidence of the very large and varied number of plants, seeds, and bulbs which we cultivate; and as the work is a very costly one we hope those who find it of use or to whom it has given some little pleasure will repay us by entrusting us with their orders, or a portion, whether large or small. On our part we are prepared to do all that in us lies to assist in beautifying the gardens of the British Empire and of those in foreign climes. For the rest we would repeat words used in our foreword for 1900:

"GARDENING HAS TRULY BECOME A POPULAR AND FASHIONABLE RECREATION amongst people of leisure and refinement; and indeed the formation of actual scenes of beauty with living subjects, abounding in interest individually, would seem to be a pleasant and worthy amusement, and as full of dignity as the portrayal of such scenes on paper or canvas. It is certainly the most healthful of hobbies; gardeners are longer lived than men of any class.

"THE TASTE FOR HARDY PERENNIAL PLANTS has increased in a very marked degree of recent years, and we are so glad to assist by any small means in our power the culture of kinds that can be grown *in the open garden at all seasons without undue expense*, that we have systematically added to our collections, from home and world-wide sources, species which will grow and thrive in this country, until our stock of this class has become the largest in the kingdom and probably in the world. As we only compile the Manual once during each year, but are continually adding to the number of species and varieties and are in communication with collectors throughout the globe, it would be wise of purchasers to inquire of us whether any plant, bulb, or seed not catalogued can be supplied before seeking elsewhere. Our country-grown roots are so large and healthy that every post brings us letters with expressions of grateful appreciation.

"OUR SEEDS, GROWN BY OURSELVES without the great additional expense entailed by city warehouses, offices, and town labour, are for these reasons reliable as well as inexpensive. We should like it to be more generally understood that we actually *grow* a very large portion of the seeds we offer; we are genuine seed growers as well as merchants, so that we can afford to sell these new, at first hand, of the very choicest quality and at the lowest prices. We are such large actual producers of seeds, plants, and bulbs, that there is no reason why we should be undersold by any firm in the United Kingdom or abroad."

EXHIBITION AWARDS TO US during the year include one Gold, six Silver Gilt, and four Silver Medals, with 22 Certificates of Merit, from the Royal Horticultural and other Horticultural Societies.

With our recommendation of this book to our customers for their careful perusal; with the assurance that all orders and inquiries shall receive courteous and efficient attention; and with our respectful greeting for the New Year,

James   Kelway.

We are, Your obedient Servants,

Kelway & Son

Farr's Hardy Plant Specialties

Edition 1915-16

tells of the favorite plants that make the hardy garden an endless joy from the earliest days of spring to the time when the plants must be covered for their winter sleep. It is a book—rather than a mere catalogue—describing in an extremely interesting way the habits, the form, the likes and dislikes of my favorite perennial plants, with notes about the time of blooming and colors of the flowers. There are many illustrations of my Irises, Peonies, Delphiniums, Aquilegias, hardy Chrysanthemums, with twelve full page plates in natural colors reproduced from Lumiere plates, just as the flowers grow here at Wyomissing.

Over Five Hundred Varieties of Peonies

are accurately described, the text having been prepared from my own field notes. The book is an authority on Irises as well as Peonies, classifying and describing the hundreds of varieties and telling how and where to grow them. Other favorite hardy plants described are the Phloxes, Asters, Poppies, a choice selection of Roses, together with a unique collection of the new and rare Lilacs.

This Book Is for You

If you write for it. I trust that it will be an inspiration to you, as its predecessors have been to others who love the many hardy plants that are a never failing source of delight to those who know them intimately.

BERTRAND H. FARR

Wyomissing Nurseries

103 Garfield Avenue   **Wyomissing, Penna.**

Examples of Bertrand Farr's advertising

136

Levi Mengel, founder and first director of Reading Public Museum, temporarily helping with beginning ground work in 1925

The Story Behind and About Dr. Stout's Daylilies

DR. A. B. STOUT

HOW TO JUDGE A DAYLILY

1—IS IT HARDY? Will it survive in sub-zero temperatures? In poor soil? In spite of neglect?

2—HOW LONG DOES IT BLOOM? The number of bloom buds to a stem equals the approximate number of days of bloom. Some Daylilies bloom for more than a month. Others for only several weeks.

3—HOW DEDENDABLY AND PROFUSELY DOES IT BLOOM? Does the plant produce a liberal number of bloom stems, with many branches and many bloom buds, year after year? Does the performance of the plant catch the eye at a distance?

4—DO THE BLOOMS AND THE STEMS HAVE GOOD SUBSTANCE? Are the blooms resistant to hot sun and to rain? Or do they curl, bleach, burn or open poorly? Do the stems remain upright and graceful regardless of winds, drought or beating rains?

5—IS THE PLANT CLEAN? Do the shriveled buds hang on to disfigure or do they drop quickly? Does the foliage remain green and upright into fall or does it sprawl or flop? Does it become "blighty" by late summer?

6—DO THE BLOOMS REMAIN OPEN EVENINGS? Top performers in this respect remain open to midnight, while new buds open. Some close before sundown. Stout Hybrids are outstanding for good evening habit. See catalog descriptions.

7—IS IT DISTINCT FROM OTHER DAYLILIES? Does it vary sufficiently in season, type, shape, pattern or color from others already existing?

NOTE: We introduce and handle all of, and only, Dr. Stout's Hybrid Daylilies. Not that they are the only good daylilies, but they have all been critically checked and tested to an unequalled extent for many years. They are distinct. They have superior garden habit. The first ones have been, and newer ones will be, outstanding and popular for many years.

Before the first World War, Dr. A. B. Stout, Director of Laboratories at the New York Botanical Garden, became interested in Daylilies; the hardiest of garden plants but then lacking in colors and good garden habit. As his studies progressed he envisioned: 1-New colors and combinations of color, 2-New and longer seasons of bloom, 3-Larger and smaller blooms, 4-Improvements in many respects for better garden show and better garden habit. He realized that such improvements in daylilies would add extremely dependable and easily maintained beauty to all types of gardens, especially through the otherwise dull summer months.

Since 1916, the New York Botanical Garden has obtained wild and varied species of daylilies from China, Mongolia, Manchuria, Siberia, Korea and Japan; also from Botanical Gardens of Europe. For more than thirty-five years Dr. Stout has hybridized these species and has applied selective and scientific breeding for numerous generations; has observed, recorded, evaluated and selected, critically and painstakingly, for good behavior in all kinds of weather, through day and night.

In this study, some 150,000 seedlings were grown, evaluated and discarded. Of these less than 100 of the most outstanding and superior individuals have been introduced, and about 300 are still being evaluated at the Farr Nursery Co.; in each case only the best of its class, and in each case, only after ten, or more, years of observation, comparison and test of the individual introduced.

The rights to, and responsibilities of, propagation and distribution, and co-operation in evaluation, were assigned to Mr. Bertrand Farr, in 1920, as a pioneer contemporary in daylily interest and enthusiasm. Shortly thereafter, Dr. Stout achieved red, pink and the other new Daylily colors. More than a thousand "New Daylilies" could have been introduced on the basis of new and gorgeous colors, new patterns, new sizes and new seasons. This has not been done because Dr. Stout and Mr. Farr regarded the "performance" of a daylily to be much more important than the beauty of the bloom. Neither does the Farr Nursery Company wish to distribute any daylily which will not be outstanding for many years to come.

As results are achieved, even if expectations are exceeded, Dr. Stout and the Farr Nursery Company do not approve for introduction, until the best acting seedling of a new class has been ascertained by years of observation and comparison. Quite often a seedling, selected years ago as most desirable, is never introduced because of improvement noted in a newer seedling.

The remaining few, and proven best, seedlings are the Daylilies which we are privileged to offer and distribute at an introductory price, which by an agreement with Dr. Stout, shall not exceed $3.00 per plant. Dr. Stout and we have refused many and all offers of $10.00 to $100.00 per plant from visitors who desired scarce or rejected seedlings. We reduce the price to less than $3.00 as soon as supply permits.

2

FARR NURSERY CO.

Bagdad

Patricia

Cinnabar

New Daylilies by Dr. A. B. Stout

This Spring we are pleased to present fourteen Daylilies developed at the New York Botanical Gardens by Dr. A. B. Stoudt.

These have been selected after sixteen years of breeding, including the development and the critical observance of more than 50,000 seedlings. They are, accordingly, desirable and distinct.

Bagdad. June-July, 42". A combination of several rich colors is its characterization. Clear orange throat. Outer parts of petals are a coppery red over orange. Veins and midzone are "madder brown". Sepals more uniform of one color. Flower is large 5", full and widely open. $3.00.

Bijou. July; 25". Distinct, small-flowered, Multiflora hybrid. Blooms are profuse, full and spread about 2½" on many branches. Ground color orange, overcast rich fulvous red with darker midzone. $3.00.

Chengtu. July-Aug., 36". Sprightly, brilliant, orange red, with a deeper velvety carmine midzone. Spread 4½". Pleasingly recurved. Exceptionally good foliage in hot dry summer. $3.00.

Cinnabar. July-Aug. 30". Fine delicate shade of brownish red sprinkled cinnamon and strongly gold-glistening. Throat is cadmium yellow. Medium large flower 5" spread. Petals and sepals recurve. Up to 18 flowers on one stem. Attractively displayed, just above foliage. Extra long season. $2.00.

Dauntless. July; 24". Yellow orange somewhat lighter than cadmium yellow. Throat greenish yellow. Pastel shades well blended. Full and medium size flower 4½". Good fragrance. $3.00.

Linda. July; 30". Golden yellow petals, cinnamon flecked in contrast with bright yellow sepals. Red eye on petal blends well with the pale pastel shades. Petals pleasingly crinkled. Large flowered, 5". $3.00.

Midas. June-July, 40". Clear, uniform glowing orange. Flowers full and spread about 5". Very tall and erect. Excellent for Perennial background. $3.00.

Mikado. June-July; 36". Flowers of striking color, the large spot of mahogany red in each petal contrasts sharply with the rich orange of the rest of the flower. Tends to bloom again during Sept. $3.00.

Multiflora Summer Hybrids. July-Aug., 30". Clear orange blooms. Numerous flowers to a scape. Long bloom period. Small to miniature blooms, 2-3" across. $3.00.

Patricia. June-July, 30". Pale yellow with tinge of lemon chrome and throat of flower greenish. Petals and sepals of uniform tone. Large flowered, 5", full, with pronounced fragrance. $3.00.

Serenade. June; 48". Very light pastel shades of yellow and red in pleasing harmony. Petals twisted and crinkled with faint halo. Flowers medium large, on tall, stiff stems. $3.00.

Soudan. June; 36". Empire yellow, broad petaled flowers, very full, with pleasingly crinkled petals and sepals. Medium large flowers, 4". A good full lily type flower. $3.00.

Vesta. July; 30". Deep orange flowers with a glistening gold sheen. Open flowers have spread of more than 4". Semi-dwarf habit. Holds up well in hot weather. $3.00.

Vulcan. July; 30". Even toned light velvety maroon, with faint golden brown midrib. Throat of the medium large flower, 4", is golden orange. $3.00.

NOTE:—The following Stout Hybrids have been withdrawn until stock has again increased to a point which permits a price not exceeding $3.00. This will hardly occur before the fall of 1938. The varieties are Charmaine, Jubilee, Majestic, Nada, Princess, Rajah, Sonny, Taruga, Theron, and Wau-Bun.

BETTER PLANTS... *By FARR*

THE BOY

In Memoriam and Retrospect

From First Farr Catalogue, 1908

I TAKE pleasure in presenting herewith the first edition of my catalogue of Hardy Plant Specialties, as it is another step toward the realization of a desire, formed many years ago, to live and be among beautiful flowers; to work among them and to be surrounded by them. The call has been instinctive and irresistible, and the complete and final surrender has brought restoration to health and a joy of living that has made it worth while, regardless of any monetary returns.

THE MAN

From "Hardy Plant Specialties"

A BOY'S garden on the prairie, far out in Iowa, which developed a passionate love of "growing things." Then the great city, with "a nameless longing" till one day my doctor said: "Go back to the country and dig." A final surrender and an utter abandonment to an absorbing passion, a man's garden that long since overflowed out into the open fields; a glorious riot of color and intoxication of delight. Peonies, Iris, Phlox—I must have them all, and for ten years I have gathered them from all over the world.

From new series catalogue "Better Plants . . . By Farr," 1922

THE title "Better Plants—By Farr," that I have adopted as my business slogan, may impress some at first as an egotistical assertion. I do not mean it in that sense; rather, it represents an ideal toward which all of us are striving, myself and the faithful associates who have grown and developed with the business here, and who, by their conscientious efforts, have helped me to the success so far achieved. The term "Better Plants" is very broad in its scope. It means better cultivation, better packing and shipping, better and more prompt service in the office, and, most important, to select for the inexperienced gardener, out of the hundreds of varieties in the trade, those which will give the most satisfactory results and the ones really worth while.

From 1924 issue "Better Plants . . . By Farr"

TO YOU, my friends and patrons, I again extend my thanks for allowing me to share with you the joy of gardening. I repeat that, to me, it means life in the fullest sense, and if I can be instrumental in adding ever so little to the beauty and happiness of the world, I feel that life is worth while.

IN ANTICIPATION

From 1924 issue "Better Plants . . . By Farr"

I AM proud of the group of energetic, loyal and progressive workers who comprise my organization. Every one of them has had many years of nursery experience. Thanks to their efforts, the formerly crammed and crowded shipping seasons are becoming less and less of a rush, in spite of a constantly increasing percentage in volume over previous years. I believe we have been able to give as nearly perfect services as it is possible for nurserymen to give. To the men who have thus helped me to convert the slogan, "Better Plants—By Farr," into an actuality, I am proud to dedicate this booklet of Hardy Plants.

THE FARR POLICY

1. To observe, select, propagate and introduce the best varieties existing among Mr. Farr's rare collection of plant varieties.

2. To persist in weeding out and discarding all but the best varieties of each group or classification.

3. To produce plants of the highest quality by propagating them after the best methods we know of, think of, hear about, or read about.

4. To lower costs and prices by efficient management. Economies introduced during 1924 now permit us to ship plants by parcel post prepaid, while Peony and Iris prices have been reduced.

5. To maintain and increase our list of regular customers by always giving satisfaction.

L. W. NEEDHAM, *General Manager*
H. G. SEYLER, *Secretary-Treasurer*

ANNA WILLIS FARR, President

Better Plants
— By Farr

Left: page from 1925 Farr Nursery Co. catalog, right: cover from Bertrand Farr's last catalog

**Second Edition
1924**

Bertrand H. Farr—
Wyomissing Nurseries Co.
Wyomissing, Penna.

Acknowledgements

Many people kindly assisted me in the preparation of this book, and I wish to acknowledge and thank them.

For my several trips to Womelsdorf, Rich Hawk was most generous in accommodating me in his Farr Nursery and Landscape Co. office, providing access to the Farr archives there, lending various materials like catalogs and glass slides, and, in general, graciously opening the way to my major source of information. His office manager Larry Bashore also made my research trips there productive and pleasant.

When Catharine Keiser Reed answers the phone and says, "Reed," I know I am about to have a charming time. Over phone conversations and personal visits, she has recalled details about the Farr nursery from her girlhood over 80 years ago – a girlhood I was so pleased to find captured in Farr catalog photographs and still alive in her spirit.

For a variety of assists from other individuals in the Berks County, Pennsylvania area, I want to thank William Kahler, Elrita Seyler, David Bausher, Merlin Kramer, George and Mary Ann Ruth, Edwin Kershner, Ben Zintak, Joan Sutton, Charles Murdough, Eleanor Kegerise, Tim Glick, Lauri Coffey, Laetitia Marshall, and Jerre Richards.

I was fortunate to have efficient and friendly help from the following librarians and libraries: Ketta Lubberstedt, Kendall Young Library, Webster City; Sherry Vance, Albert R. Mann Library, Cornell University; Stephen Sinon, Jane Dorfman and Linda DeVito, LuEsther T. Mertz Library of The New York Botanical Garden; Maureen Horn, Massachusetts Horticultural Library and Archives, and Stephanie Clark, New England Regional Depository; Stacy Stoldt, Lenhardt Library of the Chicago Botanic Garden; Barbara Brophy and her small army of volunteers, Historical Society of Berks County; Kathy Hess, Reading Public Library; and Christopher Ritter, Wyomissing Public Library.

Many officers and members of American horticultural societies generously shared by mail and by phone information and advice, for which I am very grateful. Without describing each contribution, I would like to thank all of these people for their combined help on both the history of the Farr period and current institutional history. From the American Iris Society: Anne and Mike Lowe, Clarence Mahan, E. Roy Epperson, Paul Gossett, Linda Sercus, Hal Griffey, Tracy Plotner, Gesine Lohr, Philip Edinger, Dorothy Stiefel, Anner Whitehead and Mike Unser. From the American Peony Society: Harvey Buchite, Reiner Jakubowski and Claudia Schroer. From the American Hemerocallis Society: Kevin Walik, Ken Cobb, Sydney Eddison, Gretchen Baxter, Michael Bouman and Linda Sue Barnes.

Other organizations provided important information through the courtesy of Ron Roth, Marilyn Wademan, Deborah Winkler and Vasti DeEsch at Reading Public Museum; through Greg Robertson at Pennsylvania Landscape and Nursery Association; and through Jonathan Stayer at Pennsylvania State Archives. Accountant Donald Black examined the Farr financial statements and organized them for the appendix.

When we meet to confer, designer Ellen Hardy always turns up with good ideas for the design of the book, soothes my occasional worries with her cheerful manner, and patiently accommodates changes in text or photos. I thank her for all her help with this book.

Just as my wife Pat has been for me throughout our 49 years of marriage, she certainly continued to be for producing this book – nourisher, advisor, critic, editor, nudger, sustainer. For all those roles and for her, herself, I am most grateful.

—*George H. Edmonds*

$\mathscr{Source\ Notes}$

Chapter 1 *Transformation*

13 city's business directory: *Boyd's Directory of Reading* (Reading, PA: W.H. Boyd Co., 1891). Published annually, this set of directories provided further information on Farr's 1 business and residence.

14 biographical account: Cyrus T. Fox, ed., *Reading and Berks County, Pennsylvania: A History*, (New York: Lewis Historical Publishing, 1925), 221-2.

17 deed records: County of Berks, Pennsylvania. Recorder of Deeds Office, Reading, PA.

Chapter 2 *The Early Years*

21 Farr narrates: What follows through this chapter are quotations and information from an undated, typewritten autobiography in the collection of Farr Nursery and Landscape Co., Womelsdorf, and published in the American Iris Society *Bulletin* No. 14, January 1925, pp. 3-6.

22 Bert's father's winning five prizes: *Hamilton Freeman*, Oct. 19, 1881.

23 "when Bert was a boy": From April 18,1964 letter quoted in *Iris Chronicles of the Historical Iris Robins of the American Iris Society*, No. XIII, F-3.

23 "Have You Seen Him": *Hamilton Freeman*, Sept. 4, 1878.

24 Biographical sketches: Morton Montgomery, *Historical and Biographical Annals of Berks County* (Chicago: Beers, 1909), 547. Also, Fox, op. cit.

25   Charles M. Hovey: Albert Emerson Brown, *History of the Massachusetts Horticultural Society* (Boston: Massachusetts Horticultural Society, 1927), 115 *et passim.*

30 wedding report: "Anna F. Willis – Bertrand H. Farr," *Webster City Tribune*, Sept. 11, 1896.

32 "When Carrie Cleans the Room": undated, typed manuscript in the collection of Farr Nursery and Landscape Co., Womelsdorf.

Chapter 3 *The Iris*

34   "it was really not": John C. Wister, *The Iris: A Treatise on the History, Development and Culture of the Iris for the Amateur Gardener* (New York: Orange, Judd, 1927) 33

34   "[Farr] was the first person": John C. Wister, *Better Plants,* Special Memorial Issue, Nov. 15, 1924.

34   "Juniata has probably been used": R.S. Sturtevant, American Iris Society *Bulletin* No.14, Jan. 1925.

34   "'Juniata' was a standout": Clarence E. Mahan, *Classic Irises and the Men and Women Who Created Them* (Malabar, FL: Krieger, 2007), 195.

35   "Most of the 'red' irises": Ibid., 197.

35   "All the time": Ibid., 194.

35   "The bearded iris was not": Ibid., 189.

35   "When Farr began breeding": Ibid., 195.

35   "It is *astonishing*": William J. McKee and Jamison R. Harrison, *Half Century of Iris* (Worcester, 1954) quoted in *Iris Chronicles*, F-22.

38   Mahan adds: Mahan, 193.

40   John Ravel: "18 Acres of Iris", article based on the 1929 American Iris Society "Checklist" with information provided by John Ravel. From Historical Iris Preservation Society website: www.hips-roots.com/articles/18-acres.html.

42   In another account: Sydney B. Mitchell, *Iris for Every Garden* (New York: Barrows, 1949) quoted in *Iris Chronicles*, F-22.

42   John Wister wrote: John C. Wister, *The Iris,* 33

42   Two later writers: William J. McKee and Jamison R. Harrison, quoted in *Iris Chronicles*, F-22.

Chapter 4 *The Peony*

52   "I do not even know": A.P. Saunders, "Bertrand Farr and Peonies," in American Iris Society *Bulletin* No. 14, Jan. 1925, 11.

52   In 1902 Charles W. Ward: The following information and quotations about the early history of the American Peony Society are from A.P. Saunders, "History of the American Peony Society" in James Boyd, ed., *Peonies: The Manual of the American Peony Society* (American Peony Society, 1928), 1-15.

54 "[When] in 1897": Bertrand H. Farr, "The Peony," undated, typed manuscript in the collection of Farr Nursery and Landscape Co., Womelsdorf.

58 "Mr. Farr's exhibit": *Reading Eagle*, June 11, 1920.

58 "For the delegates attending": *Reading News-Times*, June 12, 1920.

58 The Secretary of the Peony Society: American Peony Society *Bulletin* No.13, 1920, 11-24.

Chapter 5 *Phloxes, Delphiniums, Etc.*

68 Founded in 1836: Dickson Nurseries Ltd. website, www.dickson-roses.co.uk.

72 Stout writes that Farr: A.B. Stout, "Bertrand H. Farr," *Journal of the New York Botanical Garden*, Vol. XXV, 1924, 320.

73 In her book: Sydney Eddison, *A Passion for Daylilies* (New York: HarperCollins, 1992), 39

75 Founded in 1904: *Pennsylvania Landscape & Nursery Association 1904-2004* booklet, 3-5.

75 "No sane man": "Nurserymen in Annual Session," article in unnamed, undated Harrisburg newspaper in collection of Farr Nursery and Landscape Co.

Chapter 6 *Wyomissing*

Information in this chapter came from my previous book: George H. Edmonds, *Wyomissing – An American Dream: Enterprise Shaping Community* (Andover, MA: GHE Books, 2006).

Chapter 7 *The Later Years*

86 John Wister writes: John C. Wister, "Visits to Wyomissing" in American Iris Society *Bulletin* No. 14, Jan. 1925, 13.

89 Well-designed, sturdy: "J. Horace McFarland," American Academy of Park & Recreation Administration article on website maintained by Dept. of Recreation, Park & Tourism Sciences, Texas A&M University: www.rprs.tamu.edu/pugsley/McFarland.htm.

90 *Anyone who had to do:* from *Better Plants*, Special Memorial Edition, Nov. 15, 1924, 3.

92 In 1918 a letter: Correspondence between John Nolen and the Wyomissing Development Company, 1923-1932, Sept. 12, 1918. Courtesy of the Division of Rare and Manuscript Collections, Cornell University Library.

93 On May 3, 1921: Minutes of the Wyomissing Development Company, 1913-1934.

Courtesy of Hagley Museum and Library.

94 *We [here in Wyomissing]*: "City One of Most Beautiful Little Towns in the West," *Webster City Daily News*, no date, 1924.

Chapter 8 *The Last Year*

99 The founder and first director: Information from Reading Public Museum website: www.readingpublicmuseum.org.

102 Muhs concludes: Correspondence between John Nolen and the Wyomissing Development Company, September 12, 1924.

105 In 1922 Farr had shipped: "Bertrand Farr Gives Collection to This City," *Webster City Daily News*, Oct. 6, 1922.

106 Miss Izanne Chamberlain: Miss Izanne Chamberlain, "Dreams Fulfilled," American Peony Society *Bulletin* No. 27, 1926, 19.

106 *Mr. Farr was not*: Ibid.

106 "Mr. Farr was apparently": "Florist Farr Dies, Aged 61," *Reading Eagle*, October 11, 1924.

107 In Webster City: "Bertrand Farr Dies At Home In Pennsylvania," *Webster City Daily News*, Oct. 13, 1924.

110 And, finally: Bryson Hines, undated, handwritten letter to Mrs. Anna Farr, in collection of Farr Nursery and Landscape Co.

Chapter 9 *The After Years*

115 In Womelsdorf: H.G. Seyler to E.H. Fulling, letter dated Nov. 18, 1957. Courtesy of Sydney Eddison.

117 A month earlier: "1500 Shrubs And Trees Are Given Museum," *Reading Times*, March 12, 1925.

117 By 1928: "Museum to Don Flowery Garb for 'Lilac Sunday,'" *Reading Times*, May 28, 1928.

120 Through neglect: Marcus Maxon, letter in American Peony Society *Bulletin* No. 253, 1985, 39.

122 "Of all the dainty": John C. Wister, Massachusetts Horticulture Society magazine *Horti-culture*, Nov. 1, 1924, 537. Courtesy of Lenhardt Library, Chicago Botanic Garden.

123 A recent president: Mahan, 190.

Sources

American Iris Society. *Bulletin.* No.14. Jan. 1925.

———*Bulletin.* No. 30, Jan. 1929

———*Bulletin.* No. 338, July 2005

———*Iris Chronicles of the Historical Iris Robins of the American Iris Society.*
  No. XIII, Farr. Compiled by Harriet Segessemann.

American Peony Society. *Bulletin.* No.13, 1920

———*Bulletin.* No. 27, 1926

———*Bulletin.* No. 253, 1985.

Boyd, James, ed. *Peonies: The Manual of the American Peony Society.* American Peony
  Society, 1928.

Boyd's Directory of Reading. Annual editions of 1891 to 1925. Reading, PA: W.H. Boyd
  Co.

Brown, Albert Emerson. *History of the Massachusetts Horticultural Society.* Boston:
  Massachusetts Horticultural Society, 1928.

Cottage Gardens Nursery Co., Inc. *Peonies for 1908.* Queens, N.Y.: Cottage Gardens
  Nursery, 1908. Courtesy of Massachusetts Horticultural Society.

Dessert, A. *General Catalogue of Paeonies,* No. 15. *Chenonceaux:* A. Dessert, Peony
  Grower: 1905. Courtesy of Massachusetts Horticultural Society.

Eddison, Sydney. *A Passion for Daylilies.* New York: HarperCollins, 1992.

Edmonds, George H. *Wyomissing – An American Dream: Enterprise Shaping
  Community.* Andover, MA: GHE Books, 2006.

Fox, Cyrus T., ed. *Reading and Berks County, Pennsylvania: A History.* New York:
  Lewis Historical Publishing, 1925.

Farr, Bertrand H. Catalogs and newsletters issued under differing titles. First Edition,
  1908 published in Reading: Pengelly & Brother. All other catalogs, in Harrisburg:
  McFarland Publicity Service. Courtesy of Rich Hawk, William Kahler, and Albert R. Mann
  Library – Cornell University.

———*Farr's Irises, Peonies Phloxes and Hardy Plant Specialties.* First Edition, 1908.

———*Farr's Hardy Plants.* Second Edition, 1909.

    Third Edition, 1911.

    Fourth Edition, 1912

    Fifth Edition, 1915

————*Farr's Hardy Plant Specialties.* Sixth Edition. 1918
   Seventh Edition, 1920
————*Better Plants – By Farr.* First Edition, 1922-3.
   Second Edition, 1924
   Third Edition, 1925
   Unnumbered editions of 1926, 1927, 1928, 1929, 1930 and 1931.
————*Better Plants.* Newsletters. Vol. I. Nos. 1-8, Feb. to Dec. 1923.
   Vol. II. Nos. 1-6. Feb-Mar. to Nov-Dec. 1924.
Goos & Koenemann. Catalog. Nieder-Walluf, Rheingau: Goos & Koenemann, 1895.
   Courtesy of Massachusetts Horticultural Society.
Hovey & Co. Hovey's *Illustrated Catalogue of New and Rare Plants.* Boston: Hovey &
   Co., 1884. Courtesy of Massachusetts Horticultural Society.
Kelway & Son. *Kelway's Manual.* Langport, Somerset: Kelway & Son, 1902. Courtesy
   of Massachusetts Horticultural Society
Lowe, Anne. "Bertrand H. Farr – A Pioneer Irisarian" in Historic Iris Preservation
   Society ROOTS, Spring 2003.
Mahan, Clarence. *Classic Irises and the Men and Women Who Created Them.*
   Malabar, FL: Krieger, 2007
Montgomery, Morton. *Historical and Biographical Annals of Berks County.* Chicago:
   Beers, 1909.
Pennsylvania Landscape & Nursery Association 1904-2004. Harrisburg, 2004.
Stout, A.B. "Bertrand H. Farr." *Journal of the New York Botanical Garden.* Vol. XXV,
   1924.
Terry, H.A., *Choice Seedling Paeonies Originated by H. A. Terry* [catalog], Crescent,
   Iowa, 1906. Courtesy of Massachusetts Horticulture Society.
Wister, John C. "Quaker Lady." *Horticulture.* Nov. 1, 1924.
————*The Iris: A Treatise on the History, Development and Culture of the Iris for the
   Amateur Gardener.* New York: Orange, Judd, 1927.

Interviews:

Linda Sue Barnes, Wade, NC
David Bausher, Wyomissing, PA
Harvey Buchite, Anoka, MN
Ken Cobb, Raleigh, NC
Lauri Coffey, Wyomissing, PA
Sydney Eddison, Newtown, CN
Paul Gossett, Tulsa, OK
Rich Hawk, Womelsdorf, PA
Reiner Jakubowski, Waterloo, Ontario
William Kahler, Mohnton, PA
Eleanor Kegerise, Temple, PA
Merlin Kramer, Bethel, PA
Anne Lowe, Blackstone, VA
Mike Lowe, Blackstone, VA
Clarence Mahan, McLean, VA
Charles Murdough, Womelsdorf, PA
Tracy Plotner, Moralla, OR
Catharine Keiser Reed, West Lawn, PA
George & Mary Ann Ruth, Womelsdorf, PA
Claudia Schroer, Gladstone, MO
Linda Sercus, Upper Montclair, NJ
David Seyler, Lebanon, PA
Elrita Seyler, Wyomissing, PA
Dorothy Stiefel, Spencer, NY
Kevin Walek, Fairfax Station, VA
Anner Whitehead, Richmond, VA

Newspapers:

Hamilton Freeman
Reading Eagle
Reading News-Times
Reading Times
Webster City Daily News
Webster City Tribune

Websites:

American Hemerocallis Society: www.daylilies.org.

American Iris Society: www.irises.org.

American Peony Society: www.americanpeonysociety.org.

Dickson Nurseries, Ltd.: www.dickson-roses.co.uk.

Historic Iris Preservation Society: www.hips-roots.org.

Reading Public Museum: www.readingpublicmuseum.org.

World Iris Society: www.worldiris.com.

Index

About the Author

Born and raised in Wyomissing, Pennsylvania, George Edmonds has spent most of the rest of his life in Andover, Massachusetts, where he was an English teacher at Phillips Academy and a director of educational programs serving the Lawrence Boys' Club and the Lawrence Public Schools and where he now lives in retirement with his wife Patricia.

He is the author of *Wyomissing—An American Dream: Enterprise Shaping Community,* a history published in 2006 to help celebrate the centennial of the Borough of Wyomissing.